VICTORS' JUSTICE

The Tokyo War Crimes Trial

MICHIGAN CLASSICS IN JAPANESE STUDIES
NUMBER 22

CENTER FOR JAPANESE STUDIES
THE UNIVERSITY OF MICHIGAN

VICTORS' JUSTICE

The Tokyo War Crimes Trial

RICHARD H. MINEAR

CENTER FOR JAPANESE STUDIES
THE UNIVERSITY OF MICHIGAN
ANN ARBOR, MICHIGAN   2001

Reprinted in 2001 with the permission of
Princeton University Press by the
Center for Japanese Studies,
The University of Michigan,
202 S. Thayer St., Ann Arbor, MI 48104-1608

Library of Congress Cataloging-in-Publication Data

Minear, Richard H.
    Victors' Justice: the Tokyo war crimes trial / Richard H.
Minear.
        p. cm. — (Michigan classics in Japanese studies ; no. 22)
    Originally published: Princeton, N.J. : Princeton Univer-
sity Press, 1971.
    Includes bibliographical references and index.
    ISBN 1-929280-06-8 (pbk. : alk. paper)
    1. Tokyo Trial, Tokyo, Japan, 1946-1948. I. Title. II. Series.
KZ1181 .M56   2001
341.6'9—dc21
                                                        2001028237

The paper used in this publication meets the requirements
of the ANSI/NISO Standard Z39.44-1992
(Permanence of Paper for Publications and Documents in
Libraries and Archives).

Printed in the United States of America

Dedicated to the many Americans whose opposition to the war in Indochina has made them exiles, criminals, or aliens in their own land.

TABLE OF CONTENTS

PREFACE TO THE 2001 REPRINT

When *Victors' Justice* appeared in 1971, it was the only monographic treatment in Western languages of the Tokyo war crimes trial. The contrast with the Nuremberg trial was striking: libraries of material on Nuremberg, little on Tokyo. In the intervening years, we have made significant progress. There has been much fine scholarship in Japanese, and the publisher Kodansha underwrote the monumental documentary film *The Tokyo Trial* (4 hours and 37 minutes; director: Kobayashi Masaki; 1983). The basic texts of Tokyo are essential for serious study. They were not available widely in the 1960s; they are available now, edited by R. John Pritchard. The titles are: *The Tokyo War Crimes Trial: The Complete Transcripts of the Proceedings of the International Military Tribunal for the Far East in Twenty-two Volumes* (New York and London: Garland, 1981); *The Tokyo War Crimes Trial: Index and Guide,* 5 vols. (New York and London: Garland, 1981–87); and *The Tokyo Major War Crimes Trial: The Records of the International Military Tribunal for the Far East,* 124 vols. (Lewiston, N.Y.: Edwin Mellen Press, 1998–). Moreover, two monographs have added significantly to our knowledge of the Tokyo trial: *Sheathing the Sword: The Demilitarization of Japan,* by Meirion and Susie Harries (London: Hamilton, 1987), pp. 95–183; and John W. Dower's *Embracing Defeat: Japan in the Wake of World War II* (New York: Norton/The New Press, 1999), pp. 443–84. Also appearing, though adding little, were Arnold C. Brackman's *The Other Nuremberg: The Untold Story of the Tokyo War Crimes Trials* (New York:

Morrow, 1987) and Herbert P. Bix's *Hirohito and the Making of Modern Japan* (New York: HarperCollins, 2000). Brackman was a reporter on hand during the trial; despite the passage of four decades between the trial's end and the date of publication, the book has a frozen-in-amber quality, restating the premises of the prosecution essentially unchanged. Similarly, Bix allows his fixation on the emperor to dominate his view of the trial. A special case is a book that bears the name of the Dutch judge at the trial, B. V. A. Röling, author of one of the dissents: *The Tokyo Trial and Beyond: Reflections of a Peacemaker,* ed. Antonio Cassese (Cambridge, England: Polity, 1993). It is the edited transcript of a long interview in 1977. The interview, between native speakers of Dutch and Italian, presumably took place in English; it was reedited ten years later by two editors new on the scene. In 1983 at an international conference on the Tokyo trial, I spoke on "The Individual, the State, and The Tokyo Trial," and the distinguished Japanese historian Ienaga Saburō spoke on "The Historical Significance of the Tokyo Trial" (*The Tokyo War Crimes Trial: An International Symposium,* ed. C. Hosoya, Y. Ohnuma, N. Ando, R. H. Minear [Tokyo: Kodansha International, 1986], pp. 160–70). Still, there has been little fundamental challenge to the legal issues as I set them out in *Victors' Justice,* at least as they apply to the Tokyo trial.

Central to any coming-to-terms with the Tokyo trial is the figure of the Indian judge, Radhabinod Pal. His was the most thorough-going and wide-ranging dissent; it challenged both the legal basis and the procedure of the trial. It is difficult today to put ourselves back into the emotions of the immediate postwar period, in which the Tokyo trial took place. Most judges and most observers were so caught up in the war effort and its aftermath that their comments about the trial, when we read them today, seem time-bound and partisan. This is not the case with Judge Pal, who condemned the law of the trial for being retroactive and found all the defendants innocent. Ashis Nandy's "The Other Within: The Strange Case of Radhabinod Pal's Judgment on Culpability" (in Nandy, *The Savage Freud and Other Essays on Possible and Retrievable Selves* [Princeton: Princeton University Press, 1995], pp. 53–80) offers a sympathetic portrait by a family friend; indeed, it is the only treatment of Pal's background. However, attacks have been far more frequent. Brackman (p. 344) says of Pal, "the war criminals had a ringer on the bench." In the mid-1970s Ienaga Saburō and I crossed swords on the issue of Pal, Ienaga attacking and I defending (my "In Defense of Radha Binod Pal" and Ienaga's "Bias in the Guise of Objectivity" appear in *Japan Interpreter* 11.3 [Winter 1977]: 160–80). Ienaga had argued that Pal was sympathetic to the Tokyo defendants because he, like they, was strongly anticommunist; I argued that Ienaga, reading Pal in translation, misunderstood Pal's convoluted statements.

The Harries' portrait of Pal reflects British diplomatic discomfort with the implications for India of Pal's anticolonial stand at Tokyo and the antagonism toward Pal of the British judge. In *The Tokyo Trial and Beyond* Röling (p. 28), not a hostile witness, says: "[Pal] had even been involved with the Indian Army that fought with the Japanese against the British." Dower

(p. 632, n. 65) quotes Ienaga to argue that Pal was "strongly anticommunist." Bix (p. 595), footnoting Brackman, calls Pal "an outright apologist for Japanese imperialism." In "Justice Under The Sun: Japanese War Crime Trials," an article from the journal *World War II* available on the web (www.thehistorynet.com/WorldWarII/articles/0996_text.htm), Robert Barr Smith avers that Pal "*was a member* of the Indian puppet army that served the Japanese at a time when the vast majority of Indian soldiers remained true to their salt" (my italics; Barr offers no evidence). So for these critics Pal is variously "a ringer for the war criminals," "strongly anticommunist," "an apologist for Japanese imperialism," and a traitor to the British army.

That Pal was a member of the Indian National Army is utterly improbable. During the Pacific War Pal was in his mid-fifties. Beginning in early 1941, he sat as a judge on the (British) Calcutta High Court. The Indian National Army was drawn from Indian soldiers in the British military who found themselves in Japanese captivity; it operated against the Allies from bases outside of India. After the defeat, many Indian lawyers—among them Nehru—rallied to the legal defense of the first members of the Indian National Army to be tried for treason by the British. Perhaps Pal sympathized with those lawyers, and perhaps Pal commented to his fellow-judge Röling that he admired their stance. More than three decades later Röling remembered the comment, whatever it was. After two editings by different editors fifteen years apart, that comment became the statement we find in *The Tokyo Trial and Beyond*. If Pal expressed sympathy for the Indian National

Army defendants on trial by the British, it was likely after the war, and Pal was in good company.

Given the importance of the issues at stake, *ad hominem* assault on Radhabinod Pal is to be expected. So also is support from Japan's revisionist right, which sees in Pal's opinion the exoneration of Japan's prewar and wartime policies and behavior. This support creates additional suspicion about Pal among those, like Ienaga, on the Japanese left. Nevertheless, the Tokyo trial was a legal (or quasi-legal) proceeding, and we need to address it, in part at least, in legal terms, as a legal proceeding. Pal was a lawyer and judge well versed in the law, and we need to address the legal issues he raised. It should not be impossible to isolate the legal issues of the Tokyo trial from its moral and historical issues.

In 1970, in the Preface to this book, I stated: "I do not hold a brief for Tojo. I do hold a brief for justice, even to my enemies." I was paraphrasing a comment about the German Kaiser made by the legal advisor to the American delegation at Versailles in 1919. At the symposium in Tokyo in 1983 (p. 160), I began my remarks by stating: "The Tokyo trial was a flawed trial, but Japan was not without guilt." Let us give legal issues their due before coming to broader conclusions about the Tokyo trial.

The preference of scholars of international law and other commentators, scholarly or journalistic, *not* to discuss Tokyo has changed little over the past thirty years. The contrast with Nuremberg remains sharp. How can we explain this disparity? Because serious treatment of Tokyo casts doubt on major aspects of the Nuremberg trial. But nontreatment is evasion, a failure to confront the issues.

In *Requiem for a Nun,* William Faulkner wrote, "The past is never dead. It's not even past." The issues of Nuremberg and Tokyo bear Faulkner out; they are more alive now than at virtually any other time since 1948. The international community expresses outrage over atrocious acts in Cambodia, Rwanda, the former Yugoslavia, elsewhere; but what to do? Set up an international criminal court? The U.S., chief proponent of the Nuremberg and Tokyo trials, has feared subjecting U.S. citizens to a non-U.S. court—but that is precisely what Nuremberg and Tokyo did to German and Japanese nationals. Have citizens of the United States never committed atrocities abroad that went unpunished by domestic courts? Will that never happen in the future? The atomic bombing of Hiroshima and a host of more recent incidents suggest otherwise. President Bill Clinton signed on to the international criminal court tentatively, over Congressional resistance, and at the last possible moment—last possible moment both in terms of the provisions for setting up the court and in terms of his own tenure in office. It remains to be seen how the administration of President George W. Bush treats the issue. But underlying the political maneuvering surrounding the new court are the serious legal issues that Judge Pal raised at Tokyo, and these legal issues make me skeptical that the new court will succeed where Tokyo failed.

The Vietnam War is no longer the burning issue it was when I was writing this book, but the lessons I took from that war continue to guide my teaching and my scholarship.

xiv

In 1971 I owed a major debt of gratitude to R. Miriam Brokaw and Princeton University Press, who accepted this manuscript after half a dozen other commercial and university presses had rejected it. Now I thank Bruce Willoughby and the Center for Japanese Studies at the University of Michigan.

Richard H. Minear
Amherst, Massachusetts
January 2001

PREFACE TO THE FIRST EDITION

FEW Americans know much about the Tokyo trial. Most people have only a vague memory that a trial took place and that its verdict corroborated our convictions about the dastardly and criminal nature of Japan's wartime leadership and policies. My major concern in writing this book has been to challenge this prevailing image of the trial, to demolish the credibility of the Tokyo trial and its verdict. Of necessity my task has been primarily a negative one, but I hope it is not without its positive aspects. There is great value to be gained from understanding past mistakes, especially, perhaps, our own.

I write primarily for an American audience, but this book will also be read in Japan, and many of my Japanese friends will be unhappy with it. For ideological or personal reasons Japanese scholars have stayed away from the trial. Where some coverage was unavoidable, they have tended to affirm the validity of the trial and its verdict. /Apparently, they fear that denigration of the trial will lead to a positive reevaluation of Japan's wartime policies and leadership. /

The relation between denigration of the Tokyo trial and resuscitation of Japan's wartime policies and leadership is not a necessary one, but the potential for mischief is obvious. For this reason I should like here to remove any doubt among my readers—Japanese or American—about my own purposes. Paraphrasing the statement of James B. Scott, legal advisor to the American delegation at Versailles in 1919: "I do not hold a brief for Tojo. I do hold a brief for justice, even to my enemies."

The Tokyo tribunal found Tojo guilty and sentenced

him to death by hanging. It is my contention that he was legally innocent. But my brief for Tojo stops there. The Tokyo tribunal dismissed the claim that the Japanese government had been motivated by considerations of self-defense. It is my contention that considerations of self-defense played an important role. But my brief for Japan's prewar policies stops there. Many Japanese acts on the continent of Asia before and during the war are as repugnant to me as current American acts in Indochina.

Despite my attack on the trial, I have not sought for or found scapegoats. Robert H. Jackson, Joseph B. Keenan, President William Webb, General Douglas MacArthur: all of these men I have criticized sharply, but I have not made scapegoats of them. The major share of the blame for the Tokyo trial lies with the assumptions, the world-view, all these men held in common. As my final sentence states, in punishing the Japanese leaders we fooled ourselves. It is this delusion I attack, and I hope I have done so without creating new delusions. John W. Hall has written recently: "We need to rethink the causes of the Pacific war from what can only be described as a tragic view, one which takes no comfort in scapegoats and offers no sanctuary for private or national claims of moral righteousness. . . ." Professor Hall's comment I endorse entirely.

The current American concern with American war crimes in Indochina presents a second point at which misunderstanding may arise. I am fully in favor of conventional war crimes trials, as in the case of Lieutenant Calley. Such trials are essential to American honor and to the discipline and pride of American armed forces. Moreover, as Brigadier General Telford Taylor and others have suggested recently, certain American military policies in Vietnam—free-fire zones, saturation bombing, and the like —are of highly dubious legal character. Presumably, at least two American presidents and their civilian and military advisors could be held responsible. Such action I favor strongly.

But when the issue is not conventional war crimes but aggression, when it is the whole course of American policy and indeed the history of Indochina and East and Southeast Asia, then I must demur. A tribunal convened today to consider these issues might come closer to the truth than did the Tokyo tribunal after World War II. That would be child's play. But how close is close enough? And would any such judgment be truly useful? The attempt to establish legal guilt—not for atrocities, but for the war itself— would be politically convenient and satisfying. Moreover, we have today what was lacking in 1945: precedents, the precedents of Nuremberg and Tokyo and the Eichmann trial. But there are both good and bad precedents. The Tokyo trial is a bad precedent, bad enough, I suggest, to cast doubt on the Nuremberg precedent as well. The wiser course would be to return to the international law of the period before 1945, when atrocities were considered justiciable but the issue of aggression was not.

The war in Vietnam has affected all of us in one way or another. This book is in large part the result of its effect on me. Let me explain.

I attended high school and college in the 1950's. I pursued my graduate studies in the 1960's. My college generation was not noted for its activism. Graduate training further encouraged timidity: a careful, modest choice of thesis topic; constant concern for "scholarly tone" and objectivity; and a preoccupation with the non-ideological facets of scholarly life. Not only did I see no major problems in the postwar relations between the United States and Japan, but I also considered concern with problems so nearly contemporary to be journalistic, unscholarly, unhistorical. I was happy to leave the field to the political scientists, and it seemed odd that they should find it a rewarding object of study.

The war in Indochina changed all that. For one thing, it soon became obvious from my study of the American involvement there that very little about American policy was right. Could American policy be enlightened regarding Japan when it was so benighted about Vietnam? Very likely not. For another thing, my study of American policy in Vietnam raised in my mind grave suspicions about the concerns of political science, or at least of the political scientists writing on Vietnam. Samuel Huntington, Douglas Pike, Ithiel de Sola Pool, Frank Trager: surely it was not coincidental that the hawks, the ideologists, were nearly all political scientists. If American policy drew support as it did from their scholarship, then it was simply too dangerous to leave recent history—of Vietnam or of Japan—to their tender mercies.

Finally, the lack of public outcry against the Vietnam war (until very recently) represented a failure of education, a failure all the more inexcusable in a time of flourishing area studies. Area studies were flourishing, but only in the universities. Specialists talked primarily to specialists about problems of largely academic concern. The new learning of these specialists penetrated but little into the non-academic consciousness.

Vietnam turned my scholarship in a political direction. It led me to reexamine the recent history of America's relations with Japan. It encouraged me to write on a subject of interest outside the academic world. It emboldened me, once I had started on the Tokyo trial, to adopt a polemical tone.

I started on the Tokyo trial with a vague awareness that all was not right. I had read Justice Pal's dissent some years earlier, and my intention at first was to prepare a reader, a sampling of opinion about the trial designed to make Justice Pal's opinion available more widely. My intended neutrality, fraudulent from the first, dissolved as the case against the Tokyo trial emerged in its major outlines.

This book is political scholarship. It is political in its choice of subject. It is political in its tone. It is political in the implications I draw for the present day. Earlier American studies of the postwar scene were also political, but in a different way: in their very neglect of such issues as the Tokyo trial. Consider for a moment these facts. First, all the essential ingredients on which this book rests were available in 1949, twenty-two years ago. Although confined to a handful of major libraries, the records of the trial were in the public domain, accessible without special permission. Second, Justice Pal's opinion was published privately—in India, to be sure—in 1953, eighteen years ago. Third, Paul W. Schroeder published his *The Axis Alliance and Japanese-American Relations* in 1958, thirteen years ago. In that book he called for scholarly attention to the trial and expressed his own sense that the trial was a travesty. Finally, none of the essential research demanded any foreign language.

Surely there must be an explanation for this neglect of the Tokyo trial. To me it lies partly in the factors I have cited about my own graduate training. The Tokyo trial was recent history; it was peripheral to a serious and scholarly interest in the cultural and intellectual history of Japan; it was too big a topic for a fledgling graduate student to tackle. It was also a political topic, an uncomfortable one, better left alone.

Yet neglect is no solution, and errors of omission come back to haunt us. Area specialists owe it to the larger public to concern themselves at least part of the time with topics of immediate relevance to American policy. They should address themselves frequently not to their scholarly peers, but to the general public. They should deal not only with the successes that may teach us little, but also with the failures that may teach us more. Surely we know enough about the bright side of recent Japanese-American relations. It is time now to study the reverse course of the Occupation, the conclusion of the peace with Japan, the Mutual Security Pact, Okinawa. It is my hope that this study of the Tokyo trial will encourage others to turn their talents to these problems.

The Tokyo trial is a failure that can instruct us. I have written this book in the belief that an awareness of the absurdities and the inequities of the Tokyo trial will help us to rethink some of our assumptions about American policy in Asia, about Japan, and about Indochina.

For criticism of the manuscript I am indebted to: Carl Boyd, Albert M. Craig, David E. Green, Harold Josephson, Nagao Ryuichi, and Edwin O. Reischauer. George A. Furness, defense counsel at the Tokyo trial, read the manuscript with great care just before it went to press. These individuals have contributed greatly to this book. Nevertheless, the views I have expressed are mine, and I bear sole responsibility for them and for errors of fact and interpretation.

It is a pleasure to acknowledge also those who facilitated my search for materials: Philip P. Brower of the MacArthur Memorial Bureau of Archives, Norfolk, Va.; Lewis C. Coffin of the Library of Congress; Edith Henderson of the Harvard Law Library; Inoue Tadao and Toyota Kumao of the War Crimes Materials Room of the Japanese Justice Ministry; Sara D. Jackson and John Taylor of National Archives; Myres S. McDougal of the Yale Law School; Muramatsu Michio of the Law Faculty of Kyoto University; and James T. Patterson of Indiana University. The Research Foundation of the Ohio State University supported my writing during the summer of 1968. Finally, I am grateful to R. Miriam Brokaw of Princeton University Press for her unstinting efforts on my behalf.

Kyoto, May 1971   RICHARD H. MINEAR

VICTORS' JUSTICE
The Tokyo War Crimes Trial

NOTE ON JAPANESE NAMES

Japanese names throughout are given in Japanese order, that is, the family name precedes the personal name. Diacritical marks have been removed from the text but are available in the Index.

I.

INTRODUCTION

> I think we can say that to some ex-
> tent the Tojo trial itself provided
> a wholesome example of a concept
> of Anglo-Saxon justice.
> —Joseph B. Keenan, 1949

> In the last analysis, this trial was a
> political trial. It was only victors'
> justice.
> —Tojo Hideki, December 1948

THE Tokyo trial opened on May 3, 1946. At 9:30 a.m. the marshal cried: "The International Military Tribunal for the Far East is in session and is ready to hear any matter brought before it." The Tokyo trial was underway.

The opening ceremonies took place in the auditorium of the old Japanese War Ministry. This very large room had been remodeled carefully, both to give dignity to the setting and to facilitate photographic coverage of the trial. But something was not quite right. In its very first article covering the trial, *Time Magazine* compared the setting unfavorably with Nuremberg: "Nuremberg's impresarios had used simpler furnishings, relied on the majesty of the concept to set the tone." By contrast the Tokyo trial was theatre, and its klieg lights suggested "a Hollywood premiere." But premiere it was not. The Tokyo trial, wrote *Time*, "looked . . . like a third-string road company of the Nuremberg show."[1]

[1] *Time*, May 20, 1946, p. 24.

The high bench included seats for eleven justices. Each justice represented one of the nations whose allied efforts had brought Imperial Japan to defeat and the present accused to the dock. But on that opening day only nine seats were filled; two justices had not yet arrived. The same nations were also represented by associate prosecutors, who together formed an International Prosecution Section.

Across the room from the bench was the dock. The dock had seats for twenty-eight defendants. Twenty-six were present now, and the final two would arrive in time for all of them to plead innocent that afternoon. They had once been very powerful men. Fourteen of the twenty-eight had held the rank of general in the Imperial Japanese Army. Seven of these had served as War Minister; nine had held wartime commands. Most conspicuous among them was Tojo Hideki himself, Prime Minister and War Minister at the time of Pearl Harbor and during most of the war and for a short period chief of the Army General Staff to boot. The Imperial Japanese Navy was represented by three admirals. Among the civilian defendants were five career diplomats. They included Hirota Koki, Foreign Minister from 1933 to 1936 and Prime Minister from 1936 to 1937, and Shigemitsu Mamoru, Foreign Minister during 1943 and 1944. There were also three bureaucrats, one politician, and one propagandist, the ultranationalist Okawa Shumei. They had once been powerful, but stripped of their uniforms and titles and sitting in the dock, they did not look awesome. Next to their husky American M.P. guards, they seemed insignificant indeed. Some thirty-odd lawyers, all but nine of them Japanese, had assembled in their defense. The aid of more American

4

lawyers had been promised, but many had not yet arrived in Tokyo.

Sir William Webb of Australia, President of the Tokyo tribunal by order of General Douglas MacArthur, opened the proceedings on that May morning by describing an affirmation, signed beforehand by all nine justices then present, to "administer justice according to law and without fear, favor, or affection." He continued: "To our great task we bring open minds both on the facts and on the law."[2] Joseph B. Keenan of the United States, Chief of Counsel by order of President Harry S. Truman, then introduced the Indictment. Late that afternoon all defendants pleaded "not guilty."

So began the Tokyo trial. No one expected that the trial would be over soon, but few of the actors in the drama could have foreseen in May 1946 that the Tokyo trial would last fully two and one half years. Eight hundred and eighteen court sessions on 417 days; testimony from 419 witnesses and from 779 affidavits; and seven months for the justices to compose their judgment: all this would elapse before the International Military Tribunal for the Far East reconvened in the same room on November 4, 1948 to hear the verdict read and the sentences pronounced. The verdict would be guilty, though not precisely as charged. The sentences: death by hanging for seven men, including Tojo and Hirota; life imprisonment for sixteen; twenty years' imprisonment for one; and seven years' imprisonment for Shigemitsu. The propagandist Okawa had been deemed unfit for trial, and two defend-

[2] *Proceedings of the International Military Tribunal for the Far East* (mimeo; hereafter *Proceedings*), pp. 21-22.

ants had died during the long proceedings. The cases against these three had been dismissed.

1. War Crimes Trials after World War II

Trials for war crimes were a conspicuous feature of the immediate postwar world. In Europe, the Nuremberg Tribunal was only the most famous of many trials. In the Pacific as well, the Tokyo trial was only one of many. Some 5,700 Japanese were tried on conventional war crimes charges, and 920 of these men were executed.[3] But the Tokyo trial was the showpiece, for the defendants here were the leaders of the defeated Japanese state and its armed forces. These were the most illustrious defendants, and the crimes alleged against them were the most serious: not simply conventional war crimes, but crimes against peace and crimes against humanity.

But what precisely were crimes against peace and against humanity? The Allies themselves had not been sure until after Germany's defeat. Prior to 1945, Allied proclamations had called for the punishment of enemy

[3] Kojima Noboru, *Tokyo saiban*, 2 vols. (Tokyo: *Chuo koron*, 1971), II, 225. Kojima gives no source for his figures, which are substantially higher than some other figures available. (For example, *Facts on File*, IX [1949], 339H.) But Inoue Tadao of the Japanese Government's Ministry of Justice (War Crimes' Materials room) confirms the correctness of Kojima's figures. The figure for total individuals put on trial is from Inoue and cannot be fixed precisely, since some individuals underwent two or more trials.

In addition to the war crimes procedures, an administrative purge removed over 200,000 Japanese at least temporarily from political activity. John D. Montgomery, *Forced to be Free* (Chicago: University of Chicago Press, 1957), p. 26; see also Hans H. Baerwald, *The Purge of Japanese Leaders under the Occupation* (Berkeley: University of California Press, 1959).

war criminals; before 1945, "war criminals" presumably referred to men guilty of conventional war crimes, those deeds covered under the various conventions signed at The Hague and in Geneva. In 1945, however, "war criminals" took on a new meaning.

Meeting in London in the summer of 1945 to draw up a charter for the Nuremberg Tribunal, the Big Four decided that the leaders of Nazi Germany would be tried not only for conventional war crimes, but also for two new crimes: those against peace and against humanity. Crimes against peace meant ". . . planning, preparation, initiation, or waging of a war of aggression, or war in violation of international treaties, agreements, or assurances, or participation in a common plan or conspiracy for the accomplishment of any of the foregoing." Crimes against humanity were ". . . inhumane acts committed against any civilian population, before or during the war. . . ."[4] Thus, when the Nuremberg Tribunal got under way in November 1945 the Nazi leaders in the dock stood accused not only of atrocities against foreign military and civilian personnel but also of planning and waging aggressive war and of inhumane treatment "before or during the war" of German Jews.[5]

[4] Text of the Nuremberg Charter in "International Conference on Military Trials," Department of State Publication No. 3080 (Washington: U.S. Government Printing Office, 1949; hereafter *London Conference*), pp. 422-428.

[5] The Nuremberg judgment rejected the prosecution's attempt to include prewar treatment of German Jews in the category of crimes against humanity. The relevant passage of the judgment reads: "To constitute crimes against humanity, the acts relied on before the outbreak of war must have been in execution of, or in connection with, any crime within the jurisdiction of the tribunal. The tribunal is of the opinion that, revolting and horrible as many

7

The major Allied concern (China excepted) throughout World War II had been with Nazi Germany, not with Japan. It was only when the European war had ended and when the Japanese defeat was imminent that the Allies publicly announced their intention to prosecute Japanese war criminals. The Potsdam Declaration of July 26, 1945 read in part: "We do not intend that the Japanese shall be enslaved as a race or destroyed as a nation but stern justice shall be meted out to all war criminals, including those who have visited cruelties upon our prisoners. . . ."[6] Much like the early Allied pronouncements vis-à-vis Germany, the term "war criminal" presumably meant someone guilty of conventional war crimes, such as the maltreatment of prisoners of war. (The London Conference reached agreement two weeks after Potsdam.) But as at Nuremberg so at Tokyo, the enemy leaders were to find themselves under indictment primarily for crimes against peace and against humanity.

The Allies had promised stern justice, but in 1945 ". . . no treaty, precedent, or custom determined by what method justice should be done."[7] Given this situation, the Allies could choose between executive action and judicial proceedings. Great Britain's initial preference was for executive action. As one early aide-mémoire stated: ". . .

---

of these crimes were, it has not been satisfactorily proved that they were done in execution of, or in connection with, any such crime." *Trial of the Major War Criminals before the International Military Tribunal,* 42 vols. (Nuremberg, 1947-1949), xxii, 498.

[6] Text in *Judgment of the International Military Tribunal for the Far East* (mimeo, November 1948; hereafter *Judgment*), pp. 3-4; Robert J. C. Butow, *Japan's Decision to Surrender* (Stanford: Stanford University Press, 1954), pp. 243-244.

[7] Robert H. Jackson, "Preface," *London Conference,* p. v.

H.M.G. are . . . deeply impressed with the dangers and difficulties of this course [judicial proceedings], and they . . . think that execution without trial is the preferable course." Not only would a trial be "exceedingly long and elaborate" and open to being misunderstood by the general public, but also the present state of international law did not permit a full statement of Nazi transgressions. Many of these transgressions, the paper stated, ". . . are not war crimes in the ordinary sense, nor is it at all clear that they can properly be described as crimes under international law."[8]

The American position was just the reverse. The U.S. Government opposed executive action in the following words: "While it [executive action] has the advantage of a sure and swift disposition, it would be violative of the most fundamental principles of justice, common to all the United Nations. This would encourage the Germans to turn these criminals into martyrs, and, in any event, only a few individuals could be reached in this way." Consequently, while acknowledging "serious legal difficulties" surrounding a judicial proceeding, the U.S. Government favored such a course: "We think that the just and effective solution lies in the use of the judicial method. Condemnation of these criminals after a trial, moreover,

---

[8] "Aide-Memoire from the United Kingdom, April 23, 1945," in *London Conference,* p. 18. See also Samuel I. Rosenman, *Working with Roosevelt* (New York: Harper & Bros., 1952), pp. 542-545. Rosenman was Roosevelt's special envoy to the British in the spring of 1945. He reports that the British leaders were "determined in their opposition to a trial—they wanted to take the top Nazi criminals out and shoot them without warning one morning and then announce to the world that they were dead." He also reports that in 1947 Churchill expressed to him a change of heart: "I think the President was right and I was wrong."

would command maximum public support in our own times and receive the respect of history. The use of the judicial method will, in addition, make available for all mankind to study in future years an authentic record of Nazi crimes and criminality."[9]

2. *Motives Lofty and Low*

High ideals were involved in the Nuremberg and Tokyo trials. We can discern them most clearly in the words of Robert H. Jackson. Jackson played perhaps the major American role in connection with the war crimes trials, and his legal credentials were impeccable. He had been U.S. Attorney General; he was an associate justice of the Supreme Court. At the request of President Truman, Jackson took leave from the Supreme Court to be the American representative at the London Conference and then American prosecutor at Nuremberg. Consider the opening passage of Jackson's justly famous Opening Statement before the Nuremberg Tribunal:

"The privilege of opening the first trial in history for crimes against the peace of the world imposes a grave responsibility. The wrongs which we seek to condemn and punish have been so calculated, so malignant and devastating, that civilization cannot tolerate their being ignored because it cannot survive their being repeated. That four great nations, flushed with victory and stung with injury, stay the hand of vengeance and voluntarily submit their captive enemies to the judgment of the law is one of the

[9] "Memorandum to President Roosevelt from the Secretaries of State and War and the Attorney General, January 22, 1945," in *London Conference*, p. 6.

most significant tributes that Power ever has paid to Reason.

"This tribunal, while it is novel and experimental, is not the product of abstract speculations nor is it created to vindicate legalistic theories. This inquest represents the practical effort of four of the most mighty of nations, with the support of fifteen more, to utilize International Law to meet the greatest menace of our times—aggressive war. The common sense of mankind demands that law shall not stop with the punishment of petty crimes by little people. It must also reach men who possess themselves of great power and make deliberate and concerted use of it to set in motion evils which leave no home in the world untouched. It is a cause of this magnitude that the United Nations will lay before your honors."[10]

Consider for a moment some of the themes Jackson touched upon. Modern war has brought mankind to the brink of destruction. War itself must be eliminated. Since all war begins with aggression, there is always a right and a wrong side. Civilization must mobilize its resources on the side of right. International law is one of these resources.

What is international law? It is not merely a "scholarly collection of abstract and immutable principles." It must grow with the needs of the times; it must change: "Unless we are prepared to abandon every principle of growth for International Law, we cannot deny that our own day has the right to institute customs and to conclude agreements that will themselves become sources of a newer and

[10] Robert H. Jackson, *The Case Against the Nazi War Criminals* (New York: Knopf, 1946), p. 3.

strengthened International Law."[11] Like the common law, international law must evolve case by case, "at the expense of those who wrongly guessed the law and learned too late their error." The "forces of law and order" must be "made equal to the task of dealing with . . . international lawlessness."[12] This task can be met by taking two steps: by incorporating the Pact of Paris (Kellogg-Briand Pact August 27, 1928), into formal international law, and by establishing the accountability of political leaders before international law. These two steps will place international law squarely on the side of right, on the side of peace.

Moreover, the wartime alliance—the United Nations—gives great promise of establishing a new world order, a new international community. Force will yield to reason, and the world will be made safe for mankind. This is the opportunity of the day and the grave responsibility of the day. Mankind must move forward on all fronts. As Jackson states later in his address: "This trial is part of the great effort to make the peace more secure. One step in this direction is the United Nations organization, which may take joint political action to prevent war if possible, and joint military action to insure that any nation which starts a war will lose it. This charter and this trial, implementing the Kellogg-Briand Pact, constitute another step in the same direction—juridical action of a kind to ensure that those who start a war will pay for it personally."[13]

Mankind must act now; not to act is unthinkable. But Jackson himself is strongly aware of the risks of bias and error in a trial of the vanquished by the victors: "To pass

[11] *Ibid.*, p. 77.
[12] *Ibid.*, p. 87.   [13] *Ibid.*, p. 89.

12

these defendants a poisoned chalice is to put it to our own lips as well. We must summon such detachment and intellectual integrity to our task that this trial will commend itself to posterity as fulfilling humanity's aspirations to do justice."[14]

Lofty motives were involved, but so were less lofty motives. Leaders of the defeated nations stood indicted primarily for the course of action that led to World War II, for the political decisions that the Allies felt had precipitated the war. The reverse of the coin of enemy criminality was the rightness of the course pursued by the Allies in the same years. The trials were designed not only to punish wrongdoers but also to justify the right side, our side. As Robert Jackson stated at the London Conference:

"Our [the American] interest in this matter [procedure] is to see that the representations that have been made to our people that this was a criminal war and was carried out in criminal fashion are followed out by the procedure that is appropriate to trial of that kind of offense. . . . But we do not want to have a result which in the light of history will fail to justify the procedures which we have taken. We think of this as rather more than trying certain persons for some specific offenses. There is involved in this the whole Nazi drive to dominate the world. There is involved in this the basis on which the United States en-

[14] *Ibid.*, p. 7. For other important expressions of the ideals behind the Nuremberg and Tokyo trials see: Sheldon Glueck, *The Nuremberg Trial and Aggressive War* (New York: Knopf, 1946); Joseph B. Keenan and Brendan Francis Brown, *Crimes against International Law* (Washington: Public Affairs Press, 1950); and Henry L. Stimson, "The Nuremberg Trial: Landmark in Law," *Foreign Affairs Quarterly*, 25.2:179-189 (January, 1947).

gaged in its lend-lease operation, the belief that this war was illegal from its inception."[15]

Later, even more bluntly, Jackson said:

"We want this group of nations to stand up and say, as we have said to our people . . . that launching a war of aggression is a crime and that no political or economic situation can justify it. If that is wrong, then we have been wrong in a good many things in the policy of the United States which helped the countries under attack before we entered the war."[16]

[15] *London Conference*, p. 113.

[16] *London Conference*, p. 384. Consider also the exchange at the Tokyo trial during the prosecution's summation. Chief Prosecutor Keenan is speaking: "The Court has shown great patience in permitting the vituperative and insolent comments about the Hull note, a message sponsored by the President of the United States and its Secretary of State, without whose leadership not alone might these proceedings never have taken place, but the history of freedom in the world might well have been altered.

"THE PRESIDENT: Mr. Chief of Counsel, the Representative on this Court of one of the greatest and proudest nations has personally written to me commending me for protecting the Allied powers against any insult that might have been offered in this court.

"Furthermore, an associate prosecutor sent to me a leading article in a great American newspaper stating that I had protected the memory of President Roosevelt. The article referred to me as a Britain [sic]. Britains, including Australians, will always revere and protect the memory of President Roosevelt.

"MR. KEENAN: Mr. President, I had not known that any remarks contained in this part of the summation would be the subject of any comment by this Court, which has had this document for well over a week. The remark just completed in this summation states that the Court has shown great patience. I would not be able to conceive of that constituting any direct or implied criticism of any tribunal.

14

If only indirectly, Allied policy would be in the dock along with the enemy leaders.

However political in origin and in implication, judicial proceedings presumed the invocation of law. Law meant procedural safeguards for the defendants. Law also meant a determination by a panel of justices whether the acts alleged were indeed crimes before international law. The British Government had foreseen difficulties here. So also did the American Government. Consider, for example, a second passage from the memorandum of January 22, 1945 quoted above. It began by speaking of the "criminality of the German leaders and their associates," and asserted that this criminality dated back "at least as far as 1933." Consequently, "many of these atrocities" charged to the German leaders began in peacetime. The memorandum continued: "These prewar atrocities are neither 'war crimes' in the technical sense, nor offenses against international law. . . . Nevertheless, the declared policy of the United Nations is that these crimes, too, shall be punished."[17] Here the Government of the United States is proposing to prosecute actions which it concedes are not crimes.

The solution to this dilemma was to build what case could be built on international law as it existed in 1945:

"And as for President Roosevelt and his memory, Mr. President, there are many of us that think it will reach to the farthest borders of history and will not need protection in this court from myself or even the President of the Tribunal. The last thought in my mind, Mr. President, was that a representative of the Commonwealth of Australia would have any thought in any manner of slighting the memory of President Roosevelt, and I beg of you to believe that never was in my mind." (*Proceedings*, pp. 38,952-38,953.)

[17] *London Conference*, pp. 5-6.

15

for example, conventional war crimes were recognized in international law; and a case could be made that aggressive war was illegal. Where the present state of international law was unclear or unsatisfactory—as, for example, in regard to individual responsibility for acts of state—then the Big Four would codify international law in such a way that German and Japanese acts became criminal and individual enemy leaders became accountable.

At the London Conference Robert H. Jackson claimed for the Big Four this right to codify international law. In his words: "I think it is entirely proper that these four powers, in view of the disputed state of the law of nations, should settle by agreement what the law is as the basis of this proceeding, and, if I am wrong about that, I do not see much basis for putting these people on trial in a quasi-judicial proceeding."[18] In the process Jackson also asserted a highly dubious standard for that law. In a report to President Roosevelt he wrote: "We can save ourselves from those pitfalls if our test of what legally is crime gives recognition to those things which fundamentally outraged the conscience of the American people and brought them finally to the conviction that their own liberty and civilization could not persist in the same world with the Nazi power.... I believe that those instincts of our people were right and that they should guide us as the fundamental tests of criminality."[19]

Law so defined seems little different from the Nazi "law" that had aroused so much antagonism among the Allies. The law in question, an act of June 28, 1935, had held that: "Whoever commits an action which the law declares to be punishable or which is deserving of punish-

[18] *Ibid.*, p. 329.   [19] *Ibid.*, pp. 48-50.

ment according to the fundamental idea of a penal law *and the sound perception of the people*, shall be punished."[20] In both cases resort to "instincts" or to "the sound perception of the people" frees the prosecution from the necessity of demonstrating that questionable acts were in fact violations of established law.

Under these conditions it is hardly surprising to find official American spokesmen deprecating the law. To quote again from the original American memorandum of January 22: "The court may consist of civilian or military personnel, or both. We would prefer a court of military personnel, as being less likely to give undue weight to technical contentions and legalistic arguments."[21] Robert H. Jackson had much the same thing in mind in a later report to President Roosevelt: "The legal position which the United States will maintain, being thus based on the common sense of justice, is relatively simple and nontechnical. We must not permit it to be complicated or obscured by sterile legalisms developed in the age of imperialism to make war respectable."[22] During the London Conference Jackson made this comment: "I have no expectation that any rule we could formulate would avoid the criticism of some scholars of international law, for a good many of them since 1918 . . . have learned nothing and forgotten nothing."[23] At the Tokyo trial, Chief Prosecutor Keenan would contend: "The development of the art of destruction has proceeded to such a stage that the

[20] *Reichsgesetzblatt*, 1, 839, Article 1; quoted and translated in Lawrence Preuss, "Punishment by Analogy in National Socialist Penal Law," *Journal of Criminal Law and Criminology*, 26:847 (1936). Italics mine.

[21] *London Conference*, p. 8.

[22] *Ibid.*, p. 50.   [23] *Ibid.*, p. 299.

world cannot wait upon the debating of legal trivialities."
Giving Jackson's "sterile legalisms" a novel twist, Keenan
would warn also against the "mustiness of legal steril-
isms."[24]

In spite of the doubtful or unsatisfactory condition of
the law, the Allies decided to establish international military tribunals for the trial of the leaders of Germany and
Japan. Yet had there been any real chance of acquittal,
the trials would never have taken place. At least three of
the four parties to the London Conference explicitly pre-
supposed the conviction of the accused. The British Government began an early aide-memoire: "H.M.G. assume
that it is beyond question that Hitler and a number of
arch-criminals associated with him (including Mussolini)
must, so far as they fall into Allied hands, suffer the penalty of death for their conduct leading up to the war and
for the wickedness which they have either themselves perpetrated or have authorized in the conduct of the war."[25]
The Soviet representative at the London Conference
stated: "We are dealing here with the chief war criminals
who have already been convicted and whose conviction
has been already announced by both the Moscow and
Crimea declarations. . . ."[26] And Robert H. Jackson, while
attacking the assumption behind the Soviet representative's statement, nevertheless felt "bound to concede" that
"There could be but one decision in this case."[27] The pre-
sumption was of guilt, not of innocence.

[24] "Opening Statement of the Prosecution," in "Trial of Japanese
War Criminals," p. 31.
[25] Aide-Mémoire from the United Kingdom, April 23, 1945,"
in *London Conference*, p. 18.
[26] *London Conference*, pp. 104-105.
[27] *Ibid.*, p. 115.

We shall examine the Tokyo trial in the light of this spectrum of motives. Did it match the high ideal of enlisting international law in the cause of world peace? Did Power submit to Reason? Or was the Tokyo trial only barely disguised revenge? Did the victors offer the vanquished a "poisoned chalice"? If our conclusion is the latter, then we must deal also with a further question, one concerning the high ideals themselves. If the trial was indeed a travesty, was it so because a lofty aim was pursued by ignoble means? By concluding that this was the case, we may salvage the ideals. But perhaps the ideals themselves were flawed. Perhaps they themselves were partly to blame for the outcome which our title describes as "victors' justice."

II.

THE TOKYO TRIAL: CHARTER, INDICTMENT, JUDGMENT

> ... stern justice shall be meted out
> to all war criminals. . . .
> —Potsdam Declaration,
> July 26, 1945

> I do not hold a brief for the Kai-
> ser. . . . I do, however, hold a brief
> for justice, even to our enemies.
> —James Brown Scott, 1921

LONG negotiations among the Big Four at the London Conference had produced the Nuremberg Charter. No similar conference preceded the promulgation of the Tokyo Charter. Instead, the Tokyo Charter was an executive decree of General Douglas MacArthur, Supreme Commander for the Allied Powers in Japan, acting under orders from the United States Joint Chiefs of Staff.[1] The charter itself had been drawn up by Americans, primarily by Chief Prosecutor Joseph B. Keenan. America's allies were consulted only after the charter had been issued.[2] Such unilateral action might have caused major friction among the Allies. But both the United States and its Allies seem to have relied heavily on the precedent set by the Nuremberg Charter, and so the involvement of the Allies (both through the Far Eastern Commission in Washing-

[1] Solis Horwitz, "The Tokyo Trial," *International Conciliation*, 465 (November 1950), p. 480.
[2] Horwitz, "Tokyo Trial," p. 483.

20

ton and through the Allied Associate Counsel for the Tokyo trial) brought only minor changes to the original charter.[3] Each member of the Far Eastern Commission, not each signatory to the Instrument of Surrender, should have the right to nominate a justice and an associate counsel; this amendment opened the way for Indian and Filipino justices to sit on the Tokyo bench. The Supreme Commander should consult with the members of the Far Eastern Commission before exercising his power to review the tribunal's judgment and sentences.[4]

The charter as amended called for the "just and prompt trial and punishment of the major war criminals in the Far East." The offenses over which the tribunal would hold jurisdiction included crimes against peace, conventional war crimes, and crimes against humanity. Only individuals whose charges included crimes against peace were to be tried by the tribunal. Official position or the orders of a superior would not free an accused from responsibility for his acts.

Fair trial for the accused would be guaranteed by the following provisions:

—public indictments, "a plain, concise, and adequate statement of each offense charged," available in the Japanese language.

[3] The original and amended charters can be found in "International Military Tribunal for the Far East," United States Department of State Publication 2765 (Washington: United States Government Printing Office, 1947), pp. 5-16; the amended charter is in "Trial of Japanese War Criminals," United States Department of State Publication 2613 (Washington: Government Printing Office, 1946), pp. 39-44. See Appendix 1.

[4] This amendment remained "Top Secret" through the early stages of the trial. Lord Hankey, *Politics, Trials and Errors* (Chicago: Henry Regnery, 1950), p. 122.

21

—a bilingual trial, conducted in English and Japanese.

—the right of counsel freely chosen "subject to the disapproval of such counsel at any time by the tribunal." If the accused does not request counsel, the tribunal may appoint one for him "if in its judgment such appointment is necessary to provide for a fair trial."[5]

—"the right of each defendant . . . to conduct his defense, including the right to examine any witness, subject to such reasonable restrictions as the tribunal may determine."

—aid in production of evidence deemed relevant to the defense by the tribunal.[6]

Finally, the charter provided for penalties, including death, to be imposed by the tribunal subject to review "except to increase its severity" by the Supreme Commander for the Allied Powers.

The echo of Nuremberg was strong and true. The Tokyo Charter differed from the Nuremberg Charter only in a few matters reflecting the differing situation: eleven justices with no alternates instead of four justices with alternates; a chief prosecutor and ten associate prosecutors instead of four chief prosecutors; a restriction of the trial to persons charged with crimes against peace; no provision for the trial of criminal organizations; two languages (English and Japanese) instead of four.[7] Regardless of the

[5] This strange article is the product of Allied amendments of the much more sound article of the original charter.

[6] Article 9.

[7] Horwitz, "Tokyo Trial," pp. 486-488.

important differences between the European and Pacific wars, Tokyo was to be the Nuremberg of the Pacific. No conference preceded the promulgation of the Tokyo Charter, and the Tokyo Charter carefully copied the Nuremberg precedent. For these reasons the record of the London Conference stands as evidence of the intent of the Allies and their conception of international law and fair legal procedure, not only for the Nuremberg trial but for the Tokyo trial too.

Once established, the machinery of the Tokyo trial included a bench of eleven justices, one justice each from Australia, Canada, China, France, Great Britain, India, the Netherlands, New Zealand, the Philippines, the Soviet Union, and the United States. For the defense there was an international defense panel: each defendant had Japanese counsel, and the United States provided a group of American attorneys to work with the defendants and their Japanese counsel.[8]

1. The Indictment

The eleven member nations, acting through the Chief of Counsel and the Associate Counsel, brought in an indictment against twenty-eight Japanese citizens. This

[8] *Ibid.*, pp. 488-493. Article 9c, "Counsel for Accused," provided for counsel of the defendant's choice subject to the approval of the tribunal or counsel appointed by the tribunal at the request of the defendant or counsel appointed by the tribunal in the absence of such a request ". . . if in its [the tribunal's] judgment such appointment is necessary to provide for a fair trial." American counsel for all defendants (some counsel served two defendants) was provided, but only—so one report goes—" 'upon the written request of the Acting President of the Tribunal [the justice from New Zealand] . . . that it was necessary to a fair trial.' " Unnamed defense counsel, quoted in Hankey, *Politics*, p. 117.

23

indictment, largely the work of the British Associate Counsel,[9] described a "criminal, militaristic clique," dominant within the Japanese Government between January 1, 1928 and September 2, 1945, whose "policies were the cause of serious world troubles, aggressive wars, and great damage to the interests of peace-loving peoples, as well as to the interests of the Japanese people themselves." The accused had formed a conspiracy whose ". . . main object . . . was to secure the domination and exploitation by the aggressive states of the rest of the world, and to this end to commit, or encourage the commission of, crimes against peace, war crimes, and crimes against humanity as defined in the Charter of this Tribunal, thus threatening and injuring the basic principles of liberty and respect for the human personality." The accused "intended to and did plan, prepare, initiate, or wage aggressive war" against the member nations "and other peaceful nations, in violation of international law, as well as in violation of sacred treaty commitments, obligations, and assurances."[10] The accused also committed conventional war crimes and crimes against humanity.

There were 55 specific counts to the indictment: 36 represented crimes against peace, 16 represented murder ("being at the same time Crimes against Peace, Conventional War Crimes, and Crimes against Humanity"), and 3 represented conventional war crimes and crimes against humanity. Of the 36 describing crimes against peace, the first outlined a broad conspiracy over the eighteen years involved to "secure the military, naval, political, and eco-

[9] Horwitz, "Tokyo Trial," p. 498.
[10] The Indictment can be found in "Trial of Japanese War Criminals," pp. 45-63; the quotation is from pp. 45-46.

nomic domination of East Asia and of the Pacific and Indian Oceans, and of all countries bordering thereon and islands therein. . . ." The fifth count charged a conspiracy covering the same period of eighteen years whereby "Germany, Italy, and Japan should secure the military, naval, political, and economic domination of the whole world. . . ." The remaining 34 counts were broken down according to lesser versions of the first conspiracy count, according to the victims of aggression (these included the member nations of the tribunal plus Thailand, the Mongolian People's Republic, and the British Commonwealth of Nations), and according to specific groups of the accused.

This indictment, signed by each of the prosecutors "acting on behalf of" his nation, was lodged on April 29, 1946.[11] The trial opened on May 3 with the arraignment of the accused. All pleaded not guilty except one defendant (Okawa), who had been dismissed from the court to undergo psychiatric treatment.

In its first week the tribunal heard argument about two preliminary motions filed on behalf of all the accused. The first challenged the legality of the tribunal under the Potsdam Declaration and the Instrument of Surrender. The second challenged the tribunal on more fundamental grounds of international law: Was aggressive war a crime in international law? Did killing in the course of an aggressive war constitute murder? Were individuals responsible for acts of state? Four defendants submitted a third motion claiming infringement of their rights as prisoners of war. All three motions were rejected within four days. The tribunal offered no reasons for rejection at that time; these reasons were later included in its final judgment.

[11] "Trial of Japanese War Criminals," pp. 62-63.

From June 4, 1946 through January 24, 1947 the prosecution presented its case. The defense then filed motions for dismissal, asserting that the evidence did not establish the charges. Within the week, the tribunal rejected these motions. From February 24, 1947 through January 12, 1948 the defense held the floor. Thereafter the prosecution was permitted to submit evidence in rebuttal, and the defense was permitted to submit evidence in mitigation (*before* the judgment of the court). Only one defendant took advantage of this dubious privilege. Final arguments lasted until April 16, 1948.[12] By that date the transcript of the record covered 48,412 pages.

2. *The Judgment*

The tribunal rendered its judgment November 4-12, 1948. In an opinion 1,218 pages long and seven months in preparation, the tribunal rejected challenges to its own jurisdiction (15 pages), issued findings of fact on the 18-year period of Japanese history (1,053 pages), and rendered judgment (7 pages) and verdicts (82 pages) on the accused.

There had been seven challenges to the tribunal's jurisdiction. The first four (in the words of the judgment) ran as follows:

"1. The Allied Powers acting through the Supreme Commander have no authority to include in the Charter of the Tribunal and to designate as justiciable 'Crimes against Peace';

"2. Aggressive war is not *per se* illegal and the Pact of Paris of 1928 renouncing war as an instrument of national policy does not enlarge the meaning of war crimes nor constitute war a crime;

[12] Horwitz, "Tokyo Trial," pp. 502-538.

26

"3. War is the act of a nation for which there is no individual responsibility under international law;

"4. The provisions of the Charter are 'ex post facto' legislation and therefore illegal."[13]

These four challenges the tribunal was "formally bound to reject" because it found the law of the charter "decisive and binding upon it."[14] However, the tribunal did not wish to imply that the charter was binding regardless of the state of international law, and so the judgment stated: "The foregoing expression of opinion is not to be taken as supporting the view . . . that the Allied Powers or any victor nations have the right under international law . . . to enact or promulgate laws or vest in their tribunals powers in conflict with recognized international law or rules or principles thereof. In the exercise of their right to create tribunals for such a purpose and in conferring powers upon such tribunals belligerent powers may act only within the limits of international law."[15]

In support of the legality of the charter, the tribunal quoted lengthy excerpts from the Nuremberg judgment: the charter is "the expression of international law existing at the time of its creation"; the Pact of Paris made resort to war "as an instrument of national policy . . . illegal in international law"; antipathy to retroactive (*ex post facto*) legislation is "not a limitation of sovereignty but is in general a principle of justice" and the greater injustice would be to let aggressors "go unpunished."[16]

A fifth challenge had asserted that the Declaration of Potsdam concerned only conventional war crimes. The tribunal held: "Aggressive war was a crime at international law long prior to the date of the Declaration of

---

[13] *Judgment*, p. 24. [14] *Ibid.*
[15] *Ibid.*, p. 25. [16] *Ibid.*, pp. 25-26.

Potsdam, and there is no ground for the limited interpretation of the charter which the defense seek to give it."

The sixth challenge argued that killing in war is not murder. The tribunal ruled against it, holding: "If . . . the finding be that the war was not unlawful then the charge of murder will fall with the charge of waging unlawful war. If, on the other hand, the war . . . is held to have been unlawful then this involves unlawful killings not only upon the dates and at the places stated in these counts but at all placed in the theater of war and at all times throughout the period of the war."[17] Then, because the real issue was the "whole offense of waging those wars unlawfully," an issue covered in other counts, the tribunal expressed no opinion on the murder counts.[18]

The final challenge concerned the rights of prisoners of war. Here the tribunal quoted the decision of the U.S. Supreme Court on the appeal of General Yamashita, that the Geneva Convention of 1929 applied only to "judicial proceedings directed against a prisoner of war for offenses committed while a prisoner of war."[19] The judgment concluded: "The challenge to the jurisdiction of the tribunal wholly fails."[20]

In its lengthy findings on issues of fact, the tribunal upheld the interpretation of the evidence put forward by the prosecution: that there had been a conspiracy to wage aggressive wars; that aggressive wars had been waged; and that the responsible Japanese leaders had shown reckless disregard for the welfare of prisoners of war. Count 1, the

[17] *Ibid.*, p. 36.   [18] *Ibid.*
[19] *In re Yamashita*, 327 U.S. 1 (1946); quoted in *Judgment*, p. 28.
[20] *Judgment*, p. 28.

major conspiracy count, had designated as the object of the conspiracy "all countries bordering" on the Pacific and Indian Oceans. The tribunal held:

". . . we do not think the conspirators ever seriously resolved to attempt to secure the domination of North and South America. So far as the wishes of the conspirators crystallized into a concrete common plan we are of opinion that the territory they had resolved that Japan should dominate was confined to East Asia, the Western and South Western Pacific Ocean and the Indian Ocean, and certain of the islands in these oceans. We shall accordingly treat Count 1 as if the charge had been limited to the above object."[21]

Within this narrower limit the tribunal found that a conspiracy had existed; indeed, the tribunal found the conspiracy to have been in existence *before* the period covered by the indictment. The judgment saw the years after 1928 as a

". . . long struggle between the conspirators, who advocated the attainment of their object by force, and those politicians and latterly those bureaucrats who advocated Japan's expansion by peaceful measures or at least by a more discreet choice of the occasions on which force should be employed. This struggle culminated in the conspirators' obtaining control of the organs of government of Japan and preparing and regimenting the nation's mind and material resources for wars of aggression designed to achieve the object of the conspiracy. In overcoming the opposition the conspirators employed methods which were entirely unconstitutional and at times wholly ruthless. Propaganda and persuasion won many to their side, but

[21] *Ibid.*, p. 1,137.

military action abroad without Cabinet sanction or in defiance of Cabinet veto, assassination of opposing leaders, plots to overthrow by force of arms Cabinets which refused to cooperate with them, and even a military revolt which seized the capital and attempted to overthrow the government were part of the tactics whereby the conspirators came ultimately to dominate the Japanese polity.

"As and when they felt strong enough to overcome opposition at home and latterly when they had finally overcome all such opposition the conspirators carried out in succession the attacks necessary to effect their ultimate object, that Japan should dominate the Far East."[22]

The judgment then catalogued Japan's aggressions, continuing:

"These far-reaching plans for waging wars of aggression, and the prolonged and intricate preparation for a waging of these wars of aggression were not the work of one man. They were the work of many leaders acting in pursuance of a common plan for the achievement of a common object. That common object, that they should secure Japan's domination by preparing and waging wars of aggression, was a criminal object. Indeed no more grave crimes can be conceived of than a conspiracy to wage a war of aggression or the waging of a war of aggression, for the conspiracy threatens the security of the peoples of the world, and the waging disrupts it. The probable result of such a conspiracy, and the inevitable result of its execution is that death and suffering will be inflicted on countless human beings."[23]

The finding on Count 1 was the critical one. In addition, the tribunal found seven counts of aggression (against

[22] *Ibid.*, pp. 1,138-1,139.   [23] *Ibid.*, pp. 1,141-1,142.

30

China, the U.S.A., the British Commonwealth, the Netherlands, France, the U.S.S.R., and the Mongolian People's
Republic) to have been proved, and two counts of conventional war crimes. Count 5 (the conspiracy with Germany
and Italy to secure "the military, naval, political, and the
economic domination of the whole world") had not been
proved; and 44 other counts had been passed over for various reasons. There remained only the allocation of responsibility for each count among the accused.

For all but two of the accused, the verdict was "guilty
of conspiracy to wage aggressive war." Of the two who
were acquitted on this count, one, Shigemitsu, was guilty
on six other counts of aggressive war and conventional
war crimes, and the other was guilty on one count of
conventional war crimes. To be sure, no one was convicted
on all counts; but no one was acquitted on all counts either.

Seven men were condemned to death by hanging. These
included Tojo, former Prime Minister Hirota, and five
generals. All seven had been found guilty on at least one
of the two conventional war crimes' counts. (Three men
similarly guilty of conventional war crimes received lesser
sentences.) Sixteen defendants received life imprisonment.
One got twenty years' imprisonment; one, Shigemitsu, got
seven. Two defendants had died during the trial; Okawa
Shumei was still under psychiatric treatment at the time
of the judgment.[24]

[24] For a "scorecard" on the tribunal's verdict, see Appendix 3.
Kojima (*Tokyo saiban*, II, 178-185) and others have charged that
the Tokyo judgment was more Draconian than the Nuremberg
judgment. In sheer statistical terms, the picture is not simple. Death
sentences were handed down to 7 of 25 defendants at Tokyo and
to 12 of 22 at Nuremberg; life sentences to 16 at Tokyo and 3 at
Nuremberg; prison terms to 2 at Tokyo and 4 at Nuremberg. On

31

The tribunal's judgment was supported fully by eight of the eleven justices. Two of these eight filed concurring opinions dealing with specific problems.[25] The three justices who dissented each filed a separate opinion. Justice Henri Bernard of France dissented, but he would have kept silent if the majority of the tribunal had seen fit to designate their judgment a majority judgment. Instead, the majority "ultimately decided to announce its decision simply in the name of the tribunal"; and Bernard felt called upon to give his dissenting views "in fairness to the Accused." Bernard dissented on two procedural grounds and on the ground that the Japanese emperor had not been indicted.[26] Justice Radhabinod Pal of India dissented on several grounds: no conspiracy had been proved; rules of evidence had been slanted in favor of the prosecution; aggressive war was not a crime in international law; even the conventional war crimes' counts had not been proved. All accused, said Pal, were innocent on all counts.[27] Justice

---

two points the Tokyo judgment clearly was more Draconian: there were no acquittals at Tokyo and there were 3 at Nuremberg; 23 sentences of death or life imprisonment at Tokyo and only 15 at Nuremberg. These figures for Nuremberg include the death sentence passed on Martin Bormann, who was tried *in absentia*.

[25] President Webb (Australia), "Separate Opinion of the President" and Justice Jaranilla (Philippines), "Concurring Opinion."

[26] Justice Bernard (France), "Dissenting Judgment," p. 1.

[27] Justice Pal (India), "Judgment," later published under the title *International Military Tribunal for the Far East: Dissentient Judgment* (Calcutta: Sanyal, 1953), hereafter *Judgment*. Citations are to the published form, but minor discrepancies between the two versions have been resolved in favor of the original. One critic (John Alan Appleman, *Military Tribunals and International Crimes* [Indianapolis: Bobbs-Merrill, 1954], pp. 263-264) writes of Pal's dissent: ". . . [it] seems to be a translation of Ghandi's [sic] theory of passive resistance or of no resistance into judicial terminology." However, he offers no justification for this strange opinion.

B. V. A. Röling of the Netherlands dissented on the reasoning behind the finding that aggressive war was a crime —he agreed that it was a crime—and on the issue of civilian responsibility for military acts.[28]

The majority judgment alone was read in open court and so became part of the transcript. Photocopies of the text of the majority judgment were issued promptly under the title *Judgment of the International Military Tribunal for the Far East*. Only the diligent reader will discover on page 1,212 that the judgment was not unanimous and that five other opinions were filed. The dissenting judgments became part of the official record, but that record has never been published in toto. Only Justice Pal's opinion has been broadly accessible; it was published as a book by a commercial press in India.[29]

The defendants were granted ten days in which to appeal to the Supreme Commander. Then, on November 24, 1948, General MacArthur consulted with the diplomatic representatives in Japan of the nations making up the Far Eastern Commission and confirmed the sentences.[30] An appeal to the Supreme Court of the United States was dismissed for lack of jurisdiction;[31] and the men condemned to death were executed on December 23, 1948.

Justice had been done. Or had it?

[28] Justice Röling (Netherlands), "Opinion."

[29] Tanaka Masaaki (*Pa-ru hakase no Nihon muzairon* [Tokyo: Keibunsha, 1963], p. 181) alleges that the Occupation authorities blocked the publication in Japan of Justice Pal's dissent. A translation of Pal's dissent (R. Pal, *Nihon muzairon* [Tokyo: Nihon shobo]) was published on November 11, 1952. The Occupation had come to an end on April 28, 1952.

[30] Horwitz, "Tokyo Trial," p. 573. On the nature of this consultation, see below, Chapter VI.

[31] See below, pp. 169-172.

III.

PROBLEMS OF INTERNATIONAL LAW

> The charter is not an arbitrary exercise of power on the part of the victorious nations but is the expression of international law existing at the time of its creation.
> —Tokyo *Judgment*, quoting Nuremberg *Judgment*, November 1948

> It was announced proudly that new principles of justice had been discovered—by the simple process of reversing what had hitherto been accepted as an elementary principle of law. . . .
> —F.J.P. Veale, 1953

THE unsettled state of international law was a major problem of the Nuremberg and Tokyo trials. For one thing, there was no precedent for the establishment of an international military tribunal. As Robert H. Jackson wrote, Nuremberg was the "first international criminal assizes in history."[1] For another, while international law clearly recognized such crimes as piracy and the maltreatment of prisoners of war, the Allies wished to prosecute their German and Japanese enemies not simply for conventional war crimes, but also for "crimes against peace" and for "crimes against humanity." These two categories

---

[1] *London Conference*, p. 432.

34

of crime were of highly uncertain status in international law. If the prosecution wished to protect itself from the charge of *ex post facto* (retroactive) legislation, it had to argue that international conventions such as the Pact of Paris had established certain acts as crimes, or that certain acts were recognized as crimes by "all civilized nations," or that the designation of these acts as criminal was a natural and logical extension of existing principles of international law.

International law is not domestic or national law. In domestic law there is not often question as to who is sovereign, not often question as to who makes or interprets law. In international law, however, these are very real questions. In the absence of world government, who makes law and who interprets it? If "all civilized nations"—what exactly does "civilized" mean?—are party to a treaty establishing a tribunal, defining international crimes, and setting punishments for these crimes, then there are few problems. But such a treaty did not exist before 1945 and does not exist today.

The United States was convinced that the leaders of the defeated nations must be punished, but it was suspicious of punishment by executive act. For these reasons the United States persuaded the Allies that only the judicial process, with full provisions for the accused to defend themselves in open court, would establish the criminality of these men and justify any punishment meted out to them. To construct a charter for a suitable judicial process, the Big Four—France, Great Britain, the United States, and the U.S.S.R.—convened a conference at London in mid-1945. The record of that conference is a fascinating document, for the Allies found it very difficult to agree

35

even among themselves as to what constituted international law and what the terms of the charter should be. But under the pressures of time and politics, they reached agreement on the Charter for the Nuremberg Trials. This charter was later adhered to by nineteen other nations and ultimately endorsed by the General Assembly of the United Nations.[2]

As we have seen, the Tokyo Charter resembled the Nuremberg Charter closely. As at Nuremberg so at Tokyo the tribunal's judgment found the law of the charter "decisive and binding" on it. Yet both judgments also defended the charters as being "the expression of international law existing at the time of" their promulgation. What was the state of this international law?[3]

1. Conspiracy

Count 1 of the indictment read as follows: "All the accused . . . participated . . . in the formulation or execution of a common plan or conspiracy, and are responsible for all acts performed by any person in execution of such

[2] *London Conference*, p. viii. For the text of the U.N. Resolution, dated December 11, 1946, see Viscount Maugham, *U.N.O. and War Crimes* (London: John Murray, 1951), pp. 102-103.

[3] There is a voluminous literature on the subjects treated below. Much of it arouses in me the impression described by Julius Stone of a "dream world created by the blandishments of municipal criminal law analogies on the one hand, and by the formidable yearnings of all peoples for international peace and security on the other." (Julius Stone, *Aggression and World Order* [Berkeley: University of California Press, 1958], p. 145.) In the discussion that follows I have restricted myself in the main to the issues as they were argued at the London Conference and at Tokyo. As a result the arguments on both sides may appear unpolished and even simplistic, but the disability is a shared one. No matter how polished the arguments on either side, the basic conflicts remain, and these we shall examine as they developed at the Tokyo trial.

plan."[4] Why should the Allies have charged conspiracy, rather than simply the commission of the various crimes alleged? There are several reasons. In the first place, the net of conspiracy can be as wide as the prosecution wishes to make it. In the Nuremberg and Tokyo cases, it was clear that the prosecution wished to cast a very wide net indeed. Consider, for example, the words of the chief British representative at the London Conference: "What is in my mind is getting a man like Ribbentrop or Ley. It would be a great pity if we failed to get Ribbentrop or Ley or Streicher. Now I want words that will leave no doubt that men who have originated the plan or taken part in the early stages of the plan are going to be within the jurisdiction of the tribunal."[5] Nor was the net at Nuremberg limited to these men. At Tokyo, the indictment for the conspiracy counts read: "All the accused together with other persons. . . ."[6] At Tokyo, Chief Prosecutor Keenan would speak in his opening statement of ". . . the large number of persons who might properly have been charged in this indictment";[7] and one of the prosecution lawyers, writing after the trial, would explain the unwillingness of the prosecution to indict a businessman—should he be acquitted, his acquittal would be taken as a blanket condonation of the actions of the Japanese business community.[8] The obvious implication is that such men were guilty unless and until indicted, tried, and proved innocent.[9]

[4] "Trial of Japanese War Criminals," p. 47.
[5] *London Conference*, p. 301.
[6] "Trial of Japanese War Criminals," p. 47.
[7] *Ibid.*, p. 35.   [8] Horwitz, "Tokyo Trial," p. 498.
[9] Robert H. Jackson would later show some awareness of the problems raised by a conspiracy charge. In a concurring opinion in *Dennis et al. vs. United States*, Jackson described the conspiracy

37

②A second reason for charging conspiracy is that in conspiracy trials in domestic law many procedural safeguards, including rules of evidence, are relaxed.[10] That such is the case in domestic law may be a charitable explanation for the otherwise incomprehensible and inexcusable readiness with which Robert H. Jackson acquiesced in the Nuremberg Charter's provisions for evidence. (See below, Chapter IV.) These two factors the American public has seen at work recently in the already infamous Spock trial.[11]

③A third factor applied to the Nuremberg Charter (but, we may hope, not to the Spock case). The establishment of such conspiracy at the major trial at Nuremberg would greatly facilitate the prosecution of lesser enemy figures at later trials. If the existence of the conspiracy were estab-

---

law as a "dragnet device capable of perversion into an instrument of injustice in the hands of a partisan or complacent judiciary," and as "awkward and inept." Still it ". . . has an established place in our system of law" and there is ". . . no constitutional authority for taking this weapon from the Government." 341 U.S. Reports 561-579 (June 4, 1951); see pages 572 and 577 for these quotations.

[10] For a layman's discussion of rules of evidence under a conspiracy charge see Jessica Mitford, *The Trial of Dr. Spock* (New York: Knopf, 1969), pp. 61-72.

[11] *Ibid.* On the conspiracy charge Miss Mitford quotes Clarence Darrow: "It is a serious reflection on America that this wornout piece of tyranny, this dragnet for compassing the imprisonment and death of men whom the ruling class does not like, should find a home in our country." She then proceeds: "The law of conspiracy is so irrational, its implications so far removed from ordinary human experience or modes of thought, that like the Theory of Relativity it escapes just beyond the boundaries of the mind. One can dimly understand it while an expert is explaining it, but minutes later it is not easy to tell it back. This elusive quality of conspiracy as a legal concept contributes to its deadliness as a prosecutor's tool and compounds the difficulties of defending against it" (p. 61).

lished at the first trial, later tribunals could take judicial notice of that fact and concentrate solely on the issue of the involvement of later defendants in that conspiracy. The major trial at Nuremberg in fact was followed by other trials; but at Tokyo all other Class A—that is, the highest ranking—suspects, detained for the length of the Tokyo trial, were released shortly thereafter.[12] Their release is all the more inexplicable given the willingness of the Tokyo justices, a willingness greater than that of their Nuremberg counterparts, to convict on the conspiracy charge.

But what constitutes conspiracy? And is conspiracy, as opposed to the actual commission of an act, a crime in international law? This question arose even at the Lon-

[12] The *New York Times* (December 24, 1948) reported the release of all but two Class A suspects. Alva C. Carpenter, chief of the SCAP legal section, explained that the verdict in the Tokyo trial made it "highly improbable" that convictions could be obtained in these other cases. This reading of the majority judgment seems strange indeed. There is at least one indication that the decision was made much earlier and on other grounds. An Associated Press despatch of February 14, 1948—eleven months earlier—had quoted "authoritative" sources to the effect that the U.S. Government had decided to drop plans to indict twenty more Japanese leaders on "international charges of plotting the Pacific war." This decision reportedly had been reached with the recommendation of Joseph B. Keenan. The Class A suspects would instead be investigated for possible conventional war crimes charges to be brought before U.S. military courts. "Occupation attorneys said that cases might be developed against possibly a dozen" (*New York Times*, February 14, 1948). Nevertheless, all twenty men remained in custody until December 24. For many of them, imprisonment without trial (or indictment) lasted three full years. In typical fashion the Far Eastern Commission could do no more than ratify the American decision. It did so on March 16, 1949 (*New York Times*, March 16, 1949).

39

don Conference. There the British representative stated: "We have a conception of conspiracy in our law and would like to know whether you have it too." In response the French delegate spoke up: "No, we do not have that conception of conspiracy. We would have to make new law."[13]

At the Tokyo trial most issues of law were joined between Chief of Counsel Joseph B. Keenan and defense lawyer Takayanagi Kenzo. Prior to his appointment by President Truman, Keenan had been a New Deal bureaucrat and politician. President Franklin D. Roosevelt had called him "Joe the Key," presumably for his liaison work on Capitol Hill. His forte was criminal law. Before the war he had written the Lindbergh kidnapping law and served as gang-busting head of the Criminal Division of the Department of Justice. Keenan was florid of face and, as *Time Magazine* suggested, reminiscent of W. C. Fields.[14] On issues of international law Takayanagi spoke for the defense. Tall for a Japanese of his generation, and of a scholarly mien, Takayanagi was Japan's leading specialist in Anglo-American law. He had been trained in the 1910's at Tokyo Imperial University, at Harvard Law School, at Chicago, Northwestern, and London's Middle Temple. Since 1921 he had been professor at Tokyo Imperial University. Now in his late fifties, he delivered his remarks to the tribunal in English.[15]

In his opening statement Chief Prosecutor Keenan sought to define conspiracy in terms of American practice:

[13] *London Conference*, p. 296.

[14] *New York Times*, Dec. 9, 1954, p. 33; *Time*, May 20, 1946. See also Appendix 5.

[15] For biographical information on Takayanagi see *Amerika ho*, 1967.2:240-257 (December 1967).

"This offense [conspiracy] is known to and well recognized by most civilized nations, and the gist of it is so similar in all countries that the definition of it by a Federal court of the United States may well be accepted as an adequate expression of the common conception of this offense."[16]

Needless to say, Takayanagi would have none of that. The doctrine of criminal conspiracy, he argued, is "a peculiar product of English legal history."[17] In support of this argument Takayanagi cited several Western legal scholars, among them Francis B. Sayre. Sayre wrote of conspiracy: "It is a doctrine as anomalous and provincial as it is unhappy in its results. It is utterly unknown to the Roman law; it is not found in modern Continental codes; few Continental lawyers ever heard of it." Not only is it peculiar to English law, continued Sayre, but it is also dangerous. Takayanagi quoted Sayre further: "Under such a principle everyone who acts in cooperation with another may some day find his liberty dependent upon the innate prejudices or social bias of an unknown judge. It is the very antithesis of justice according to law."[18]

[16] "Trial of Japanese War Criminals," pp. 8-9. The case to which Keenan refers is *Marino vs. the United States*, 91 Fed. 2nd, 691; 113 A.L.R. 975.

[17] Kenzo Takayanagi, *The Tokio Trials and International Law* (Tokyo: Yuhikaku, 1948), p. 14. This book consists of Takayanagi's two lengthy addresses to the Tokyo Tribunal, with slightly polished Japanese translations.

[18] Francis B. Sayre, "Criminal Conspiracy," 35 *Harvard Law Review*, 1922, pp. 427, 413; quoted in Takayanagi, *Tokio Trials*, pp. 15, 16. The principle to which Sayre refers in the second quotation (Takayanagi fails to specify it) is "that a criminal conspiracy includes combinations to do anything against the general moral sense of the community." Sayre argues that any definition so vague com-

Takayanagi's reasoning won the support of two justices, Pal of India and President Webb of Australia. Like Takayanagi, Pal referred to Sayre. Pal went on to assert that conspiracy had never been a part of international law. He concluded: "After giving my anxious thought to the question I have come to the conclusion that 'conspiracy' by itself is not yet a crime in international law."[19] President Webb agreed. International law, he wrote, "does not expressly include a crime of naked conspiracy." The Tokyo Tribunal "has no authority to create a crime of naked conspiracy based on the Anglo-American concept." For the tribunal to create such a crime "would be nothing short of judicial legislation."[20]

Keenan's reasoning won the support of the majority. The majority held that there was such a crime in international law. It held further that the existence of the conspiracy charged in Count 1—that is, of "the accused together with other persons"—had been proved. It held finally that twenty-three of the twenty-five defendants were guilty of complicity in that criminal conspiracy. Two of these twenty-three defendants would be found guilty *only* of conspiracy and sentenced to life imprisonment.[21]

2. The Responsibility of Individuals before International Law

As at Nuremberg so at Tokyo the charter of the tribunal asserted: "Neither the official position, at any time, of an

---

pletely robs the law of its predicability: "Once rob the law of this predicability, and the state reverts to a government by men rather than by law" (p. 412).

[19] Pal, *Judgment*, p. 574.
[20] President Webb, "Separate Opinion," pp. 8-9.
[21] See "scorecard," Appendix 2.

42

accused, nor the fact that an accused acted pursuant to order of his government or of a superior shall, of itself, be sufficient to free such accused from responsibility for any crime with which he is charged...."[22] Once again, it is easy to see why the Allies wished to establish individual responsibility for acts of government. Only by doing so could they hope to prosecute the wartime leaders of Germany and Japan. But what was the state of international law on this issue?

At the London Conference the French delegate argued that individuals could not be held responsible for acts of state. Said he: "It may be a crime to launch a war of aggression on the part of a state that does so, but that does not imply the commission of criminal acts by individual people who have launched a war...." To this the British delegate countered: "Don't you imply that the people who have actually been personally responsible for launching the war have committed a crime?" But the French delegate held his ground: "We think that would be morally and politically desirable but that it is not international law."[23]

Even Robert H. Jackson admitted difficulties: "... I am frank to say that international law is indefinite and weak in our support on that, as it has stood over the recent years." True frankness would have required the admission that international law on this point was definite, was the reverse of the position Jackson was putting forward, and had been so not merely "over the recent years" but for a much longer time; but let that be. Jackson continued: "This definition [a Soviet proposal on Article 6] seems to

[22] Article 6.
[23] *London Conference*, p. 297.

43

me to leave the tribunal in the position where it could be argued, and the tribunal might very reasonably say, that no personal responsibility resulted if we failed to say it when we are making an agreement between the four powers which fulfils in a sense the function of legislation. I think there is greater liberty in us to declare principles as we see them now than there would be in a court to use new principles that we had failed to declare in an organic act setting up the court." Failure to declare principles "as we see them now" would leave the issue to "determination by . . . the court," a prospect Jackson viewed with obvious distaste.[24]

In his opening statement at the Tokyo trial, Chief Prosecutor Keenan referred to two decisions of the U.S. Supreme Court to argue that ". . . individuals may be punished by a military tribunal for violations of international law, which, even though never codified by an international legislative body, have been sufficiently developed and crystalized to make them cognizable by courts of justice."[25] Having looked for precedents, however, Keenan admitted that there were none: "The personal liability of these high-ranking civil officials is one of the most important, and perhaps the only new question under international law, to be presented to this tribunal. That question is being squarely presented."[26] Later in the same speech Keenan was even more explicit: ". . . individuals are being brought to the bar of justice for the first time in history to answer personally for offenses that they have committed while acting

[24] *Ibid.*, p. 331.
[25] "Trial of Japanese War Criminals," p. 20. The decisions Keenan specifies are those of *Ex parte Quirin* (317 U.S. 1) and *In re Yamashita* (327 U.S. 1).
[26] *Ibid.*, p. 21.

44

in official capacities as chiefs of state. We freely concede that these trials are in that sense without precedent. And we are keenly conscious of the dangers of proceeding in the absence of precedent, for tradition crystallized into precedent is always a safe guide. However, it is essential to realize that if we waited for precedent and held ourselves in a straitjacket by reason of lack thereof, grave consequences could ensue without warrant or justification. . . . Today we are faced with stark realities involving in a certain sense the very existence of civilization."[27]

In rebutting the prosecution's argument, Takayanagi called the concept of individual responsibility for crimes against peace "perfectly revolutionary." "It is the general principle of the law of nations," argued the Japanese lawyer, "that duties and responsibilities are placed on states and nations and not on individuals." Espionage, piracy, and the like are exceptions to the "general rule of the immunity of individuals." This immunity is both a legal principle and a practical necessity of statecraft.[28]

Alone among the justices, Justice Pal held that individuals were not liable to prosecution for acts of state. Such liability would be possible, wrote Pal, only if the nations involved accepted in principle a limitation on the "sovereign right of non-intervention." For Pal, the question was not whether the Japanese leaders had comported themselves "badly . . . and thus brought their own nation to grief, but whether thereby they made themselves answerable to the international society."[29] Pal referred to the findings of the Allied Commission of Responsibilities at Ver-

[27] *Ibid.*, p. 31.
[28] Takayanagi, *Tokio Trials*, pp. 59, 60, 63.
[29] Pal, *Judgment*, p. 71.

sailles in 1919, in particular, to the dissenting report filed by the two American representatives. That report stated in part: "The American representatives are unable to agree with this conclusion [that 'all persons belonging to enemy countries, however high their rank . . . are liable to criminal prosecution'] . . . insofar as it subjects Chiefs of States to a degree of responsibility hitherto unknown to . . . international law, for which no precedents are to be found in the modern practice of nations."[30] Pal examined the argument of the prosecution and of various Western and Russian legal scholars before concluding: "That the individuals comprising the government and functioning as agents of that government incur no criminal responsibility in international law for the acts alleged."[31] In his concurring opinion Justice Delfin Jaranilla of the Philippines as much as conceded Pal's point, but then he argued that "a precedent in accordance with law and justice is [can be, should be] laid down where there exists none."[32]

The majority judgment found that individuals could be held responsible for acts of state. As the only support of its finding, the judgment offered a quotation from the Nuremberg judgment: "The principle of international law which under certain circumstances protects the representatives of a state cannot be applied to acts which are condemned as criminal by international law. The authors of these acts cannot shelter themselves behind their official

[30] "Violation of the Laws and Customs of War: Reports of the Majority and Dissenting Reports of American and Japanese Members of the Commission of Responsibilities, Conference of Paris, 1919," Carnegie Endowment for International Peace (Division of International Law), Pamphlet 32 (Oxford: Clarendon, 1919), p. 65.

[31] Pal, *Judgment*, p. 104.

[32] Justice Jaranilla, "Concurring Opinion," p. 22.

46

position in order to be freed from punishment in appropriate proceedings."[33]

3. Aggressive War

Counts 6 through 36 of the indictment charged the accused Japanese leaders with planning and preparing, initiating, and waging wars "of aggression" and wars "in violation of international law, treaties, agreements, and assurances."[34] These counts did not concern conventional war crimes committed in the course of the war. They concerned instead the nature of the war. This nature, they charged, was aggressive.

At the London Conference the criminality of aggressive war, as apart from conventional war crimes committed in the course of war, was important primarily to the American side. As Robert H. Jackson argued there: "Germany did not attack or invade the United States in violation of any treaty with us. The thing that led us to take sides in this war was that we regarded Germany's resort to war as illegal from its outset, as an illegitimate attack on the international peace and order. And throughout the efforts to extend aid to the peoples that were under attack, the justification was made by the Secretary of State, by the Secretary of War, Mr. Stimson, by myself as Attorney General, that this war was illegal from the outset and hence we were not doing an illegal thing in extending aid to people who were unjustly and unlawfully attacked. No one excuses Germany for launching a war of aggression because she had grievances, for we do not intend entering into a trial of whether she had grievances. If she had real

[33] *Judgment*, p. 25.
[34] "Trial of Japanese War Criminals," pp. 49-55.

47

grievances, an attack on the peace of the world was not her remedy. Now we come to the end and have crushed her aggression, and we do want to show that this war was an illegal plan of aggression."[35] The United States lacked the traditional justifications for going to war, and yet the United States had joined the fight against Germany. The legal formula Jackson put forward was of a piece with his concept of world peace and order, but it also represented a request for international approval of recent American policy. The only surprising thing, perhaps, is that Jackson himself linked the two so closely.

But is aggressive war a crime at international law? Before the London Conference, the British Government admitted serious doubt. In its aide-memoire of April 23, 1945, it stated: "Reference has been made above to Hitler's conduct leading up to the war as one of the crimes on which the Allies should rely. There should be included in this the unprovoked attacks which, since the original declaration of war, he has made on various countries. These are not war crimes in the ordinary sense, nor is it at all clear that they can properly be described as crimes under international law."[36] At the London Conference the French argued that they could not: "We do not consider as a criminal violation the launching of a war of aggression. If we declare war a criminal act of individuals, we are going farther than the actual law. We think that in the next years any state which will launch a war of aggression will bear criminal responsibility morally and politically; but on the basis of international law as it stands today, we do not believe these conclusions are right. . . . We do not want criti-

[35] *London Conference*, pp. 383-384.   [36] *Ibid.*, p. 19.

cism in later years of punishing something that was not actually criminal, such as launching a war of aggression."[37]

The American Government urged at the London Conference that aggressive war was a crime. But only one year earlier the Americans had been on the other side of the fence. The legal committee of the United Nations War Crimes Commission had discussed the issue in 1944, concluding that aggression was a crime; but the Commission itself had not adopted this position, "the feeling prevailing that the Governments would be reluctant to go so far."[38] Instead, the matter was referred to a subcommittee of four, representatives of Great Britain, Czechoslovakia, the Netherlands, and the United States. Of these four, only Czechoslovakia dissented from the majority report which held that:

"Acts committed by individuals merely for the purpose of preparing for and launching aggressive war, are . . . not 'war crimes.' However, such acts and especially the acts and outrages against the principles of the laws of nations and against international good faith perpetrated by the responsible leaders of the Axis Powers and their satellites in preparing and launching this war are of such gravity that they should be made the subject of a formal condemnation in the peace treaties. It is desirable that for the future penal sanctions should be provided for such grave outrages against the elementary principles of international law."[39]

[37] *London Conference*, p. 295.

[38] United Nations War Crimes Commission, *History of the United Nations War Crimes Commission* (London: Her Majesty's Stationery Office, 1948), p. 181.

[39] *Ibid.*, pp. 182, 184-185.

This report and the Czech dissent were the subject of discussion on the part of the whole commission. Though the representatives of Australia, China, New Zealand, Poland, and Yugoslavia supported the Czech position, the United States held fast, as did France, Great Britain, the Netherlands, and Greece. The matter was left to be referred to the member nations for instructions, but no resolution was ever adopted. Only one year before the London Conference, three of the Big Four had gone on record that aggressive war was not in itself a crime.

In his opening statement at the Tokyo trial, Chief Prosecutor Keenan asserted that ". . . the question of aggressive war has been considered by so many nations and deliberately outlawed by them that their unanimous verdict rises to the dignity of a general principle of international law." In support of this contention Keenan cited the first (1899) and third (1907) Hague Conventions, the Geneva Protocol for the Pacific Settlement of International Disputes, a unanimous resolution to the same effect by the League of Nations in 1927, the Sixth International Conference of American States of 1928, and the Pact of Paris. He concluded: "Acting in conformance with the demands of the public conscience of the world, by 1928 all the civilized nations of the world had by solemn commitments and agreements recognized and pronounced wars of aggression to be international crimes and had thus established the illegality of war as a positive rule of international law."

Speaking for the defense, Takayanagi directed the court's attention to the very same international covenants cited by the prosecution. His discussion of the Pact of Paris was typical. Having asserted that the intent of parties to an international treaty is essential evidence in interpreting such a treaty, Takayanagi quoted statements of intent from several parties to the Pact of Paris. For the American side he quoted Secretary of State Frank B. Kellogg. Speaking on April 28, 1928 before the American Society of International Law, Secretary Kellogg rejected categorically the notion that the American draft of the pact "restricts or impairs in any way the right of self-defense." That right of self-defense, continued Kellogg, "is inherent in every sovereign state and is implicit in every treaty. Every nation is free at all times and regardless of treaty provisions to defend its territory from attack or invasion and it alone is competent to decide whether circumstances require recourse to war in self-defense."[40] Testifying before the Senate Committee on Foreign Relations, Kellogg was even more categorical: "I knew that this government, at least, would never agree to submit to any tribunal the question of self-defense, and I do not think any of them [the other governments] would."[41] That committee reported the pact to the U.S. Senate in the following unequivocal terms: "The committee reports the above treaty with the understanding that the right of self-defense is in no way curtailed or impaired by the terms or conditions of the treaty. Each nation is free at all times and regardless

[40] The relevant portions of Secretary Kellogg's speech are reproduced in U.S. Department of State, *Treaty for the Renunciation of War* (Washington: U.S. Government Printing Office, 1933), pp. 57-59. The speech became an important item in the negotiations, incorporated (as here) into the official U.S. note of June 23, 1928, and referred to by several parties to the negotiations. Quoted in Takayanagi, *Tokio Trials*, pp. 30-31.

[41] U.S. Congress, Senate, Committee on Foreign Relations, *General Pact for the Renunciation of War*, Hearings, 70th Congress, 2nd Session, December 7, 11, 1928, p. 4. Quoted (in slightly incorrect form) in Takayanagi, *Tokio Trials*, p. 31.

of the treaty provisions to defend itself, and is the sole judge of what constitutes the right of self-defense and the necessity and extent of the same. The United States regards the Monroe Doctrine as a part of its national security and defense."[42] Takayanagi presented evidence of similar interpretation and intent on the part of the British (who spoke of "certain regions of which the welfare and integrity constitute a special and vital interest for our peace and safety"[43]) and the French.

In a note to the American chargé d'affaires of July 20, 1928, the Japanese Foreign Minister referred to Secretary Kellogg's speech of April 28 and informed him that Japan's interpretation of the pact was ". . . substantially the same as that entertained by the Government of the United States."[44] The Japanese Privy Council's report on the pact, dated June 26, 1929, stated: "Upon receipt of the proposal made by the American Government, the Imperial Government adopted the broader interpretation that the operations of national self-defense were not confined to actions to be taken for defending the territory of our own country, but extended to actions which might be adopted by the Empire in order to safeguard its vital rights and interests in China, especially in the regions of Manchuria and Mongolia, but regarded it as more opportune to re-

[42] U.S. Congress, Senate, Committee on Foreign Relations, Executive Report No. 1, 70th Congress, 2nd Session, January 15, 1929; text in *Congressional Record*, LXX, pt. 2, p. 1,730. Quoted in Takayanagi, *Tokio Trials*, p. 32.

[43] British note of July 18, 1928, in *Treaty for the Renunciation of War*, p. 73. Quoted in Takayanagi, *Tokio Trials*, pp. 33-34.

[44] Text in *Treaty for the Renunciation of War*, pp. 80-86. Quoted in Takayanagi, *Tokio Trials*, pp. 34-35.

frain from making such a declaration on this occasion."[45] Takayanagi concluded that the Pact of Paris, keystone of the prosecution's argument that aggressive war was illegal, had not limited the right of self-defense, had not confined self-defense to the defense of one's own territory, and had not envisioned or provided for a tribunal to weigh claims of self-defense.[46]

This line of argument impressed three justices. Justice Bernard of France rejected the prosecution's reading of the Pact of Paris, but he then supplied an alternative route to the conclusion that aggressive war was illegal. Justice Bernard appealed to natural law. "There is no doubt in my mind," he wrote, "that such a war of aggression is and always has been a crime in the eyes of reason and universal conscience—expressions of natural law upon which an international tribunal can and must base itself to judge the conduct of the accused tendered to it."[47]

Justice Röling of the Netherlands reviewed the evidence and found that " 'crimes against peace' were not regarded true crimes before the London Agreement . . ." But then Röling like Bernard supplied another rationale for concluding that aggressive war was illegal. He conceded to the victorious Allies the right to create such a crime even after the fact. But such crimes were of a special order, "acts comparable to political crimes in domestic law, where the decisive element is the danger rather than the guilt, where the criminal is considered an enemy rather than a villain, and where the punishment emphasizes the political measure rather than the judicial retribution. In this sense

---

[45] Takayanagi, *Tokio Trials*, p. 35.   [46] *Ibid.*, pp. 36-37.
[47] Justice Bernard, "Dissenting Judgment," p. 10.

should be understood the 'crime against peace,' referred to in the charter. In this sense the crime against peace, as formulated in the charter, is in accordance with international law."[48]

Only Justice Pal of India rejected outright the contention that aggressive war was illegal. He concluded that after the Pact of Paris "the preexisting *legal* position of war in international life remained unaffected." Wrote Pal: "So long as the question whether a particular war is or is not in self-defense remains unjusticiable, and is made to depend only upon the 'conscientious judgment' of the party itself, *the Pact fails to add anything to the existing law*." What was the state of the law, customary or statutory? "In my opinion, no category of war became illegal or criminal either by the Pact of Paris or as a result of the same. Nor did any customary law develop making any war criminal. Indeed: When the conduct of the nations is taken into account the law will perhaps be found to be *that only a lost war is a crime*."[49]

The majority judgment held that aggressive war was a crime. Once again the majority relied on a quotation from the Nuremberg judgment: "The question is what was the legal effect of this pact [the Pact of Paris]? The Nations who signed the pact or adhered to it unconditionally condemned recourse to war for the future as an instrument of policy and expressly renounced it. After the signing of the pact any nation resorting to war as an instrument of national policy necessarily involves the proposition that such a war is illegal in international law; and that those who

[48] Röling, "Opinion," pp. 44, 48.
[49] Pal, *Judgment*, pp. 48, 44-45, 59.

54

plan and wage such a war, with its inevitable and terrible consequences, are committing a crime in so doing."[50]

4. Aggression Defined

A corollary to the question of the criminality of aggressive war is the question: can aggression be defined?[51] The Pact of Paris had not tried to define aggression. The Allies at the London Conference did try, but with little success. The American attempt at London to define aggression was designed to limit the scope of the trial. As Robert H. Jackson said: "There is a very real danger of this trial being used . . . for propaganda purposes. . . . It seems to me that the chief way in which the Germans can use this

[50] *Judgment*, p. 25.

[51] The most convenient summary of the attempts to define aggression is Julius Stone, *Aggression and World Order: A Critique of United Nations Theories of Aggression* (Berkeley: University of California Press, 1958). Stone's analysis and stance are very impressive. Consider, for example, his skepticism that a definition would be helpful even if it were feasible: "To stake so much on a verbal formulation which still has to be interpreted and applied by the very organs [i.e., member-states of the U.N.] whose unreliability is the reason for the formulation, is to seek salvation in shadows" (p. 25). To be sure, Stone is not without an opposition. There is a whole literature on the subject of distinguishing permissible coercion from impermissible coercion. Most noteworthy is Myres S. McDougal and Florentino P. Feliciano, *Law and Minimum World Public Order: The Legal Regulation of International Coercion* (New Haven, Conn.: Yale University Press, 1961). For compelling criticism of McDougal and Feliciano, see Anthony D'Amato, book review, 75 *Harvard Law Review*, 458 (1961); Richard A. Falk, book review, 10 *American Journal of Comparative Law*, 297 (1961); and Richard A. Falk, *Legal Order in a Violent World* (Princeton: Princeton University Press, 1968), pp. 80-96.

forum as a means of disseminating propaganda is by accusing other countries of various acts which they will say led them to make war defensively. That would be ruled out of this case if we could find and adopt proper language which would define what we mean when we charge a war of aggression."[52] The United States suggested the following definition: "An aggressor ... is that state which is first" to declare war, to invade another state, to form a naval blockade, or to provide support for insurgent groups. Here Jackson placed heavy emphasis on chronological priority. The definition concluded: "No political, military, economic, or other considerations shall serve as an excuse or justification for such actions; but exercise of the right of legitimate self-defense, that is to say, resistance to an act of aggression, or action to assist a state which has been subjected to aggression, shall not constitute a war of aggression."[53] For Jackson the essential criminal element was the use of force; domination by peaceful means was wholly legal. When was resort to force not illegal? In two cases: self-defense and assistance against aggression. Self-defense

---

[52] *London Conference*, p. 273.

[53] *Ibid.*, p. 294. It is instructive to compare Jackson's definition with the Soviet Draft Definition of 1933. The Soviet proposal began: "The aggressor . . . shall be considered that State which is the first to take any of the following actions. . . ." Its second paragraph began: "No considerations whatsoever of a political, strategical, or economic nature . . . shall be accepted as justification of aggression as defined in Clause 1." (Text in Stone, *Aggression and World Order*, pp. 34-35.) Conspicuous by its absence is the qualification concerning self-defense and collective defense. Wrote Stone in 1957: The Soviet draft definition ". . . has run the gauntlet of a quarter of a century and of two world security organisations, without achieving either assured life or certain death" (Stone, *Aggression and World Order*, p. 34).

56

was not new or controversial; but the same could not be said about assistance against aggression. It had not been included in the Pact of Paris. It had not been mentioned in 1944 when the U.N. War Crimes Commission discussed aggression. But it had an obvious and compelling logic: it justified the actions of two of the Big Four—the U.S. and the Soviet Union—which were otherwise of dubious character in terms of international law.

The Russian delegate at London, General I. T. Nikitchenko, felt that definition of the term aggression was unnecessary. He said: "The policy which has been carried out by the Axis powers has been defined as an aggressive policy in the various documents of the Allied nations and of all the United Nations, and the tribunal would really not need to go into that. . . . The fact that the Nazi leaders are criminals has already been established. The task of the tribunal is only to determine the measure of guilt of each particular person and mete out the necessary punishment— the sentences."[54] The only definition acceptable to the Russians would have specified that aggression was something Nazi Germany had committed. Because of this disagreement and because the French insisted that defining crimes was beyond the jurisdiction of the London Conference, the charter included no definition of aggression.

In his opening statement, Chief Prosecutor Keenan satisfied himself with offering three definitions of aggression. The first two came from Webster's New International Dictionary (second edition, unabridged, 1943): "A first or unprovoked attack, or act of hostility. . . . A nation that refuses to arbitrate or to accept an arbitration award, or any other peaceful method, in the settlement of a dispute

[54] *London Conference*, p. 303.

57

but threatens to use force or to resort to war."[55] His third definition he attributed to James T. Shotwell: "The aggressor being that state which goes to war in violation of its pledge to submit the matter to peaceful settlement, having already agreed to do so."[56] Keenan did not specify which definition he wished to invoke against the Tokyo defendants.

The majority judgment completely ducked the issue of defining aggression. (So had the judgment of the Nuremberg tribunal.) The Tokyo majority's sole reference to the whole question of definition came during its discussion of the Japanese attacks of December 7, 1941. It stated: "They were unprovoked attacks, prompted by the desire to seize the possessions of these nations. Whatever may be the difficulty of stating a comprehensive definition of 'a war of aggression,' attacks made with the above motive cannot but be characterized as wars of aggression."[57] Definition apparently should proceed by the study of individual cases, not by any concrete formulation. We may not know what aggression is, but we do know that Germany and Japan committed it.

Justice Röling offered different reasons for neglecting to define the crime. The wars the Japanese fought "come within the scope of illegal aggression, whatever definition might be given." The Japanese leaders might have been motivated in part by considerations of self-defense, but

[55] "Trial of Japanese War Criminals," p. 15.
[56] James T. Shotwell, *War as an Instrument of National Policy* (New York: Harcourt Brace, 1929), p. 58; quoted in "Trial of Japanese War Criminals," p. 15. The wording is Shotwell's, but the definition (as Shotwell states clearly) is not; it comes from the Treaty of Locarno and the Geneva Protocol of 1924.
[57] *Judgment*, p. 994.

that is not really the point. Wrote Röling: "Insight in the genesis of the crime has but limited importance, as it is not so much retribution for the offense by punishment of the perpetrators which is here being sought, as a measure for protection by elimination of dangerous persons." (See above, pp. 53-54, for Justice Röling's discussion of the political nature of the crime of aggression.) Indeed, definitions would hinder the matter: "Even in a trial lasting more than two years it is well nigh impossible to write the exact story of 17 years of world history. It would be advisable not to approach a factual situation which has not been clarified in its smallest details with a legal concept which is of such subtlety that it would require those details in its application."[58] Only a broad definition is desirable, but Röling does not offer one.

Justice Pal disagreed. He disagreed, first, with the idea that no definition was necessary. "No term," he wrote, "is more elastic or more susceptible of interested interpretation, whether by individuals, or by groups, than aggression."[59] Nor are there dependable guides for even the most objective tribunal to follow. He disagreed, secondly, with all definitions suggested by the prosecution, concluding: "Perhaps at the present stage of the International Society the word 'aggressors' is essentially chameleonic and may only mean 'the leaders of the losing party.' "[60] And yet def-

[58] Röling, "Opinion," p. 50.
[59] Pal, *Judgment*, pp. 111-112. Pal might have quoted Secretary Kellogg's comment to the Senate Committee on Foreign Relations: ". . . if I had started out to define what aggression was and what self-defense was, I would not have been able to negotiate a treaty during my lifetime or that of anybody present here." *General Pact for the Renunciation of War*, p. 16.
[60] Pal, *Judgment*, p. 121.

59

inition is absolutely necessary: "One of the most essential attributes of law is its predicability [quality of being predicable, assertable]. . . . The excellence of justice according to law rests upon the fact that judges are not free to render decision based purely upon their personal predilections and peculiar dispositions, no matter how good or wise they may be. To leave the aggressive character of war to be determined according to 'the popular sense' or 'the general moral sense' of the humanity is to rob the law of its predicability."[61]

Justice Pal disagreed, finally, with the unstated philosophy behind the attempt to define aggression and to outlaw war. To outlaw war was to freeze the *status quo*: "I am not sure if it is possible to create 'peace' once for all, and if there can be *status quo* which is to be eternal. At any rate in the present state of international relations such a static idea of peace is absolutely untenable. Certainly dominated nations of the present day *status quo* cannot be made to submit to eternal domination only in the name of peace. International law must be prepared to face the problem of bringing within juridical limits the politico-historical evolution of mankind which up to now has been accomplished chiefly through war. War and other methods of *self-help by force* can be effectively excluded only when this problem is solved, and it is only then that we can think of introducing criminal responsibility for efforts at adjustment by means other than peaceful."[62] It was impossible to define aggression fairly without considering the merits of the status quo to be frozen by outlawing war, and yet no one proposed taking *that* step.[63]

[61] *Ibid.*, pp. 111-112.   [62] *Ibid.*, pp. 114-115.
[63] Compare here Stone (*Aggression and World Order*, p. 86): ". . . legal definition pre-requires a theory which shall comprehend

5. Retroactivity (Ex Post Facto Character)

A cardinal principal of domestic criminal law is that there shall be no retroactive legislation. This principle, enshrined in Article 1 of the American Constitution, is sometimes expressed in the Latin phrase: *nullum crimen sine lege, nulla poena sine lege* (unless there is a law, there can be no crime; unless there is a law, there can be no punishment). An act that was not criminal at the time of commission cannot be reached by retroactive legislation. To be sure, in countries with common-law traditions there has always been some degree of retroactivity, at least in judicial legislation: law is made case by case, determined by the judge.[64] However, to the extent that the law of Nuremberg and Tokyo was made not at Nuremberg and Tokyo but in London, it is not a case of judicial legislation analogous to the role of judges in the development of the common law. The conferees at London were not judges (although the Soviet representative became a Nuremberg judge and the French representative the alter-

a larger context than the acts of putative aggressors, wide enough, in particular, to embrace men's 'legitimate aspirations,' meaning their demands and the norms whereby these are to be judged and legitimised. There can, in other words, be no theory of aggression except as part of the theory of the 'rights' of States *de lege ferenda* as well as *lata*; and no operable definition of it save one which is based on a minimum of mutual acceptance of such 'rights.' A theory of international aggression must be a theory of social force, physical as well as other."

[64] Robert H. Jackson caught this distinction nicely in one of his last opinions as Associate Justice of the Supreme Court: "The *ex post facto* provision of our Constitution has not been held to protect the citizen against a retroactive change in decisional law, but it does against such a prejudicial change in legislation." Jackson dissent, *U.S. vs. Harris et al.*, 347 U.S. Reports 635 (June 7, 1954).

nate French judge); they were, instead, official representatives of their governments.

That the United Nations faced a problem with regard to this principle was clear at the London Conference. The discussions there over the issues of conspiracy, individual responsibility, and aggression indicated that the state of international law was highly uncertain on these basic issues of definition. Only conventional war crimes were unquestionably part of international law.

At the London Conference Robert H. Jackson argued that defining the law was within the jurisdiction of the conference. He said: "Our basic purpose is that article 6 [listing the crimes to come under the jurisdiction of the tribunal] should settle what the law is for the purposes of this trial and end the argument. . . ." If the crimes were not defined in the charter, thought Jackson, the tribunal might well find the accused guilty of the acts but hold that the acts themselves were not crimes. Said Jackson: "That we think would make the trial a travesty."

The French delegate quickly took Jackson to task. He said: ". . . there is a difference in saying that, if they are convicted in . . . those criminal acts, they will be dealt with as major war criminals, and declaring those acts are criminal violations of international law, which is shocking. It [declaring those acts to be criminal violations] is a creation by four people who are just four individuals— defined by those four people as criminal violations of international law. Those acts have been known for years before and have not been declared criminal violations of international law. It is *ex post facto* legislation. . . . It is declaring as settled something discussed for years and settling a question as if we were a codification commission." Jackson's response was as follows: "But we are a codification commission for the purposes of this trial as I see it. That is my commission as I understand it."[65] In spite of the French objection the Nuremberg Charter in its final form read: "The following acts shall be deemed criminal violations of international law, and the tribunal shall have power and jurisdiction to convict any person who committed any of them on the part of the European Axis powers."[66] The Tokyo Charter was almost identical. It read: "The following acts . . . are crimes coming within the jurisdiction of the tribunal for which there shall be individual responsibility."[67]

As we have seen, Justice Pal held that "crimes against peace" did not exist before 1945. He concluded that the Allied Powers had no authority to rewrite international law and then to apply it retroactively. Wrote Pal: "The so-called trial held according to the definition of crime *now* given by the victors obliterates the centuries of civilization which stretch between us and the summary slaying of the defeated in a war. A trial with law thus prescribed will only be a sham employment of legal process for the satisfaction of a thirst for revenge. It does not correspond to any idea of justice." Having discussed the Nuremberg judgment on this point, Pal concluded: "Whatever view of the legality or otherwise of a war may be taken, victory does not invest the victor with unlimited and undefined power now. International laws of war define and regulate the rights and duties of the victor over the individuals of the vanquished nationality. In my judgment, therefore, it is beyond the competence of any victor nation to go beyond

[65] *London Conference*, pp. 329-330.
[66] Nuremberg Charter, Article 6. [67] Tokyo Charter, Article 5.

63

the rules of international law as they exist, give new definitions of crimes, and then punish the prisoners for having committed offense according to this new definition."[68]

As we have seen, Justice Röling held that "crimes against peace" did not exist before 1945. He concluded, however, that the Allied powers did have the right to formulate new rules. He wrote: "If the principle of 'nullum crimen sine praevia lege' were a principle of *justice*, the tribunal would be bound to exclude for that very reason every crime created in the charter ex post facto, it being the first duty of the tribunal to mete out justice. However, this maxim is not a principle of justice but a rule of policy, valid only if expressly adopted. . . ." Being "an expression of political wisdom," not "a principle of justice," the *ex post facto* principle was "not necessarily applicable in present international relations. . . . This maxim of liberty may, if circumstances necessitate it, be disregarded even by powers victorious in a war fought for freedom."[69] The tribunal could not question the wisdom of the decision to disregard this principle, but Justice Röling's phraseology seems to indicate his personal antipathy. Feelings aside, Justice Röling's argument is at least straightforward. The charter was retroactive, but retroactivity was permissible.

Not so the Tokyo judgment. The majority judgment found the charter and its definition of crimes "decisive and binding"; and it held that the Allies had acted "within the limits of international law" in establishing the charter. But it offered two conflicting justifications for this finding. First, it argued at length that international law included all the crimes listed and defined in the charter. If this was the case, there was no ground for raising the issue of ret-

[68] Pal, *Judgment*, pp. 17, 30.   [69] Röling, "Opinion," pp. 44-45.

roactivity. But then, as if unsure of its first justification, the majority offered a second. This justification was the reverse of Justice Röling's. Quoting the Nuremberg judgment the majority held: "The maxim 'nullum crimen sine lege' is not a limitation of sovereignty but is in general a principle of justice. To assert that it is unjust to punish those who in defiance of treaties and assurances have attacked neighboring states without warning is obviously untrue for in such circumstances the attacker must know that he is doing wrong, and so far from it being unjust to punish him, it would be unjust if his wrong were allowed to go unpunished."[70] Principle of justice, expression of political wisdom, or limitation of sovereignty—whatever the maxim was, only Justice Pal summoned it to the support of the Tokyo defendants.

Retroactivity was not an issue, the majority judgment asserted, because the law of the charter was good international law. But even if that were not the case the charter was valid. By arguing twice the majority revealed its own uneasiness about the state of international law. It revealed also its ultimate deference to the power of the Allies to define the law as they saw fit. It was Justice Jaranilla who made all this explicit. Once a justice accepted appointment to the tribunal he ". . . unconditionally accepted not only the validity of the charter and of all its provisions, such as the definition of crimes against peace, the individual responsibility therefor, etc., but also the duties imposed upon him by the charter 'for the just and prompt trial and *punishment* of the major war criminals in the Far East.'" Jaranilla elaborated: "For instance, the charter has defined that an aggressive war is a crime and has provided that

[70] *Judgment*, pp. 23-24, 25-26.

those guilty of it are individually liable. . . . May the members of the tribunal, deriving their functions *solely* from the said charter, say that said aggressive war is not a crime and that those who waged it should not be personally liable? With due respect, such a position, in my opinion, seems absurd."[71] Abdication of judicial responsibility could hardly be more blatant.

From Justice Röling came stern rebuke: "According to the majority judgment, the tribunal, though called upon to mete out justice, is not the authority called upon to judge whether the victorious powers have stayed within the bounds of international law. . . . This standpoint seems to be not only dangerous for the future, but incorrect at this moment." Röling continued: "It would be the worst possible service this tribunal could render to the cause of international law if it should establish as a rule that an international tribunal, *called upon to mete out justice,* would have to apply the rules laid down by the Supreme Commander of the victorious nations, without having either the power or the duty to inquire whether it was applying rules of justice at all."[72] Justice Röling's concern was shared by Justice Pal, and it would later win the support of Associate Justice William O. Douglas of the U.S. Supreme Court. Wrote Justice Douglas of the Tokyo tribunal: "It took its law from its creator and did not act as a free and independent tribunal to adjudge the rights of petitioners under international law. As Justice Pal said, it did not therefore sit as a judicial tribunal. It was solely an instrument of political power."[73] On this point as on

[71] Jaranilla, "Concurring Opinion," pp. 29, 31. Italics in original.
[72] Röling, "Opinion," pp. 4-5.
[73] 338 U.S. Reports 215 (June 27, 1949). See also below, pp. 170-171.

other points, Justices Pal and Röling were free to write their dissents, but they were powerless to alter the reasoning of the majority.

6. Negative Criminality

None of the defendants at Tokyo was accused of having personally committed an atrocity. Such offenders were prosecuted, and over nine hundred of them were condemned to die, in separate tribunals. Rather, the defendants at the Tokyo trial were accused on three other counts: that they conspired to "order, authorize, and permit" Japanese officials "frequently and habitually to commit" breaches of the laws and customs of war (Count 53); that they actually "ordered, authorized, and permitted" such acts (Count 54); and that they "deliberately and recklessly disregarded their legal duty to take adequate steps to secure the observance and prevent breaches" of the laws and customs of war (Count 55)—negative criminality. Count 54 was borrowed from Nuremberg; Count 55 was new at Tokyo, almost an admission of the difficulty of convicting these defendants under Count 54.

Speaking for the defense, Takayanagi reminded the tribunal that in 1919 the American members of the Commission of Responsibilities at Versailles had opposed the doctrine of negative criminality. In their dissent to the Commission's report Robert Lansing (then Secretary of State) and James Brown Scott had forcefully attacked the concept that an official could be held liable for having "abstained from preventing . . . violations of the laws or customs of war." They had written: "To this criterion of liability the American representatives were unalterably opposed. It is one thing to punish a person who committed, or, possessing the authority ordered others to commit an

67

act constituting a crime; it is quite another thing to punish a person who failed to prevent, to put an end to, or to repress violations of the laws or customs of war. In one case the individual acts or orders others to act, and in so doing commits a positive offense. In the other he is to be punished for the acts of others without proof being given that he knew of the commission of the acts in question or that, knowing them, he could have prevented their commission."[74]

Takayanagi argued further that no evidence supported the charge of direct orders to commit war crimes. He quoted Chief Prosecutor Keenan's words: "These murders followed such a wide range of territory and covered such a long period of time, and so many were committed after protests had been registered by neutral nations, that we must assume only positive orders from above; those accused here in this prisoners' dock made them possible." This charge, argued Takayanagi, was based "on assumption and assumption only." He continued: "But it must surely be shown at what exact level the assumed command issued; and indiscriminate assumption of guilt at all levels or at all above a certain level would be essentially contrary to justice and would be revolting to the conscience of the world."[75]

The majority judgment would dismiss Count 53: ". . . we hold that the charter does not confer any jurisdiction in respect of a conspiracy to commit any crime other than a crime against peace."[76] Justice Pal did make such a finding: "no part of the charges of conspiracy" of Count 53

[74] "Violation of the Laws and Customs of War," p. 72.
[75] Takayanagi, *Tokio Trials*, pp. 56-57.
[76] *Judgment*, p. 35.

had been established.[77] In his discussion of Counts 54, and 55, Pal agreed that atrocities had taken place. The evidence, he wrote, was "overwhelming" that the Japanese armed forces had grossly mistreated enemy civilians and prisoners of war. However, Pal continued: "The question is how far the accused before us can be made criminally responsible for such acts."[78] Had there been orders, authorizations, permissions as alleged in Count 54? Pal argued that there was "absolutely no evidence of any order, authorization or permission" regarding maltreatment of civilians and no evidence that maltreatment of prisoners of war was the policy of the government. Differing attitudes toward surrender and the overwhelming numbers of prisoners of war in Japanese hands: these considerations alone, argued Pal, would explain what maltreatment did occur. Furthermore, those immediately responsible had already been tried in other proceedings. Pal concluded: ". . . it must be said in fairness to the accused that one thing that has not been established in this case is that the accused designed to conduct this war in any ruthless manner." Pal did think that Tojo was responsible for ordering the employment of prisoners of war, but this act, argued Pal, was an act of state for which Tojo should not bear criminal responsibility.[79]

On Count 55 Justice Pal argued that deliberate and reckless disregard of duty constituted no crime even under the charter. He wrote: "There is, indeed, some difficulty in reconciling Count 55 with the provisions of the charter. The charter lists as crime only 'violations of the laws or customs of war.' It does not list as crime 'disregard' of

[77] Pal, *Judgment*, p. 595.　　　[78] *Ibid.*, p. 609.
[79] *Ibid.*, pp. 620, 640, 649-651, 662, 669.

'legal duty' to take adequate steps to secure the observance of and to prevent the breaches of the laws of war. If Count 55 be taken to mean that 'the deliberate and reckless disregard of legal duty' itself constitutes a crime, then the crime charged therein would be outside the provisions of the charter and as such, outside our jurisdiction." However, Pal held that evidence of disregard might be invoked to support a charge of violating the laws of war, but in that case: "The charge will not be established till the act of violation is established to be the act of the accused."[80] In other words, Count 55 could not constitute a separate count, but evidence introduced under Count 55 could be used to support Count 54. Nevertheless, it was Pal's conclusion that on the evidence none of the accused could be found guilty of either Count 54 or Count 55.

Justice Bernard affirmed the existence of negative criminality but sought to narrow its scope. Only those who "could have prevented" atrocities yet "did not do so" could be held guilty. This finding presumably meant that no civilian could be convicted on Count 55. As to the responsibility of military men, Justice Bernard objected to the assumption that if atrocities occurred the highest military officers were responsible. He wrote: "To state as a principle as did the majority that Army or Navy commanders can, by order, secure proper treatment and prevent ill-treatment of prisoners, appears to me contrary to all the known facts of experience." He insisted on proof in each case, not simply of acts of omission, but of intent and effect.[81]

[80] *Ibid.*, p. 600.
[81] Bernard, "Dissenting Judgment," pp. 15-16.

Justice Röling also sought to narrow the scope of negative criminality. He did so by stressing three elements: knowledge, power, and duty. Only those directly responsible for the problem—for example, the Home Ministry for civilian internees in Japan proper—should be liable to prosecution under Count 55. By Röling's reasoning three men whom the majority found guilty on Count 55 should have been acquitted. They included Hirota Koki and Shigemitsu Mamoru.[82]

Although it dismissed the conspiracy count, the majority judgment held that negative criminality did exist, and that crimes under that count (and under Count 54, "ordering, authorizing, and permitting" war crimes) had been established against ten defendants. Five defendants, all generals, were convicted on Count 54 (the only order was Tojo's directive to employ prisoners of war); and all five were sentenced to death. Five additional defendants, three generals and two civilian foreign ministers, were found guilty only on Count 55. Sentences for these men on this and other counts ranged from death to seven years' imprisonment. Count 55 cost two of these men their lives.

Defendant Hirota, innocent on Count 54, was found guilty on Count 55. He had been foreign minister during the rape of Nanking (1937-1938). The majority admitted that Hirota had taken up the matter of atrocities with the War Ministry. But Hirota had accepted "assurances" from the War Ministry in spite of reports that the atrocities were continuing. "The tribunal is of opinion that Hirota was derelict in his duty in not insisting before the Cabinet that immediate action be taken to put an end to the atrocities,

[82] Röling, "Opinion," pp. 59-61, 178ff.   [83] *Judgment*, p. 1,144.

failing any other action open to him to bring about the same result."[84] Hirota's penalty—he was found guilty also of conspiracy to commit aggression—was death. General Matsui Iwane, commanding officer of the Japanese forces in Central China during the Nanking incident, was acquitted on Count 54 and all other counts except Count 55; he too was sentenced to die.

Five fundamental questions of international law lay at the center of the Tokyo trial. The state of the law on these five issues was at best uncertain. The issue of conspiracy had arisen before only at Nuremberg. There the judgment convicted only 8 of 22 defendants as against the conviction of 23 of 25 at Tokyo. The issue of individual responsibility even the prosecution admitted to be an innovation. Official representatives of the American Government at Versailles in 1919 had rejected any such liability for acts of state; so also did the French representative at London in 1945. Was aggressive war a crime? No, said the United States and Great Britain in 1944 and France in 1945. Was the Tokyo Charter *ex post facto*? Yes, said the French in 1945. Did negative criminality exist? No, said the United States in 1919.[85]

[84] *Ibid.*, pp. 1,160-1,161.

[85] The law of Nuremberg and Tokyo has been the subject of several discussions at the United Nations since 1945. On December 11, 1946 the General Assembly affirmed unanimously the "principles of international law recognized by the Charter of the Nuremberg Tribunal and the Judgment of the Tribunal." This affirmation took place while the Tokyo trial was underway. In 1947 the General Assembly directed its International Law Commission to prepare a draft code of crimes against peace. The commission's report, completed in 1950, was then sent to member governments for their reaction. Twenty years later no final action has taken place. (*cont.*)

These issues were the heart of the Tokyo case. The tribunal's majority judgment settled all in favor of the position of the prosecution, a position energetically advanced but logically vulnerable. To decide any single issue the other way would have changed the whole case radically. But the majority judgment sided with the prosecution on all. It rejected the prosecution's interpretation of international law on only one point, and that one was relatively insignificant: the criminality of conspiracy to commit conventional war crimes. Its reasoning in rejecting such criminality was important: the charter had not conferred jurisdiction over any such crime. The majority judgment asserted that the Tokyo Charter was merely declarative of existing international law. However, the evidence would seem to justify the inference that the majority judgment accepted the Tokyo Charter as "decisive and binding" regardless of the previous state of international law.

In late 1967 the General Assembly established a special committee on the question of defining aggression. The proposal had come from the Soviet Union. Observers placed five of the nations that participated at Tokyo among the abstainers: Australia, the Netherlands, New Zealand, United Kingdom, and the United States (Ambassador Arthur Goldberg had spoken out against the proposal). That committee has not reported yet. (J. N. Hazard, "Why Try Again to Define Aggression?" *American Journal of International Law*, 62:701-710 [July 1968]).

IV.

PROBLEMS OF LEGAL PROCESS

> ... in this very courtroom will be
> made manifest to the Japanese
> people themselves the elements of
> a fair trial which, we dare say,
> perhaps they may not have en-
> joyed in the fulness—in all of their
> past history.
> —Chief Prosecutor Keenan,
> May 1946

> The trial of the vanquished by the
> victors cannot be impartial no
> matter how it is hedged about
> with the forms of justice.
> —Senator Robert A. Taft,
> October 5, 1946

SUBSTANTIVE issues of international law were important to the Tokyo trial. So also were problems of legal
process. Procedural matters are always important. As
Judge Charles E. Wyzanski, Jr., has written: "If there is
one axiom that emerges clearly from the history of consti-
tutionalism and from the study of any bill of rights or any
charter of freedom, it is that procedural safeguards are the
very substance of the liberties we cherish."[1] Some procedural issues at Tokyo seem quite obvious to observers not
trained in the law, and yet these issues will find lawyers
divided: for example, the selection of the justices or the

[1] Charles E. Wyzanski, Jr., *Whereas—A Judge's Premises* (Boston: Little, Brown, 1965), p. 178.

74

choice of the accused. Other issues at Tokyo must be obvious also to those trained in the law: for example, the rules of evidence. The author of this book is a historian, not a lawyer, and his criterion of fairness may differ somewhat from that espoused by many lawyers. Yet many of my observations are supported by lawyers involved in the trial: not only the defense counsel and Justice Pal, but also Justice Bernard and Justice Röling and President Webb. Further, they are supported by many specialists in this field.

I shall discuss four issues: the selection of justices, their rules of operation, the selection of the defendants, and the rules of evidence.

1. The Selection of the Justices

The original American Charter for the Tokyo trial called for five to nine justices, one each from those signatories to the Instrument of Surrender who wished to participate.[2] The intervention of the Far Eastern Commission forced the inclusion of two more justices, one from India and one from the Philippines. The inclusion of these justices constituted a departure from the principle that the nations forming the tribunal should have been sovereign states during the Pacific war; neither India nor the Philippines had been a sovereign state before 1945 and Indian independence would not be a reality until August 15, 1947. (On the ground that the Philippines before 1945 were an American colony, the Tokyo judgment dismissed the separate count of the indictment that charged aggression against the Philippines.)[3] But the principle that stood firm was that the justices were nationals of the countries that

[2] "Trial of the Japanese War Criminals," p. 5.
[3] *Judgment*, pp. 1, 143-1,144.

75

had suffered from Japanese military activity. There were no justices from neutral nations. There was no Japanese justice.

The question of including justices from neutral or even from enemy nations did not arise at the London Conference. Rather, it was assumed that there would be four justices at Nuremberg, one each from the nations of the Big Four. The original American memorandum to President Roosevelt had suggested seven justices, one each from the Big Four and three to be selected from among the other Allies adhering to the charter.[4] But by April 1945 the United States had dropped the idea of having more than four judges.[5] The London Conference did not consider whether nationality constituted a bias, although in the discussion of rules of conduct, Robert H. Jackson indicated his expectation that the nationality of the justices might play a role. He said: "I suggest that a formula [on conduct] might be found which could be adequate to admonish judges who, after all, are nationals of our own countries and equally interested with ourselves in keeping the trials on the level that would not quite so brazenly invite accusations against us all."[6]

All the justices at the Tokyo trial came from the victor nations. This apparent onesidedness may explain the first act of the nine justices who were present at the opening of the trial. Meeting in chambers before formally opening the

[4] "Memorandum to President Roosevelt from the Secretaries of State and War and the Attorney General, January 22, 1945," in *London Conference*, pp. 7-8.

[5] "American Draft of Definitive Proposal, Presented to Foreign Ministers at San Francisco, April 1945," in *London Conference*, p. 26.

[6] *London Conference*, p. 102.

trial, the justices signed "a joint affirmation to administer justice according to law, without fear, favor, or affection."[7] This is the description of President Webb; the affirmation itself was never released. Nine justices promised in writing to do what justices are supposed to do, regardless.

The defense challenged the court on this very point. Speaking for all the defendants, Defense Counsel George Furness argued: ". . . the members of this tribunal being representatives of the nations which defeated Japan and which are the accusers in this action, a legal, fair, and impartial trial is denied to these accused by arraignment before this tribunal. . . . The question of jurisdiction is a question of moral judgment."[8] Furness made it clear that the principle involved was simply that of nationality. He said: "We say that the members of this tribunal are representatives of the nations who are parties plaintiff, nations who are the accusers. They are the representatives of those nations as are the prosecutors who were appointed by the same nations. We say that regardless of the known integrity of the individual members of this tribunal they cannot, under the circumstances of their appointment, be impartial; that under the circumstances this trial, both in the present day and in history, will never be free from substantial doubt as to its legality, fairness, and impartiality."[9]

The tribunal rejected this and all other challenges to its jurisdiction, reserving a statement of reasons until later.[10] The final judgment dealt with seven such challenges, but it did not address itself to the challenge raised by Furness. Had it done so, it might well have adopted the reasoning put forward by Chief Prosecutor Keenan, not at the trial

[7] *Proceedings*, p. 21.   [8] *Ibid.*, pp. 196-197.
[9] *Ibid.*, p. 200.   [10] *Ibid.*, p. 319.

77

itself but in his subsequent book on the subject. Wrote Keenan: ". . . the nine nations signing the Instrument of Surrender . . . were acting for the international community. The right of the world community to punish Japan's war criminals existed before the signing of the Surrender Terms and prior to Japan's acceptance of them. The Surrender Terms gave the nine signatories the right to act for all of international society, not simply for themselves."[11]

Three justices discussed what the majority did not. Justice Jaranilla argued that military commissions were composed normally of officers of the victor army. He argued further that the Potsdam Proclamation and the Instrument of Surrender "do not impose any limitation or condition whatever under which the trial . . . can or should be carried out." Hence, "Japan . . . cannot now validly object to what has been performed in accordance with the Instrument of Surrender."[12] But the objection did not come from Japan. It came from individual defendants on trial for their lives.

Justice Bernard found the provision of a trial instead of summary punishment "sufficient proof of the good-will of the Allies." He concluded: "The fact that the authors of the charter were precisely the victors and that only the government leaders of the defeated nations could be prosecuted could not be taken into consideration either. . . ." There follows then a very enigmatic remark. Wrote Bernard: "The political non-organization of the world is to be blamed for the fact that a decision prior to the trial—

[11] Joseph B. Keenan and Brendan Francis Brown, *Crimes Against International Law* (Washington: Public Affairs Press, 1950), pp. 39-40.
[12] Jaranilla, "Concurring Opinion," pp. 17, 13-14.

78

the one excluding the eventual proclamation of the responsibility of the conquerors—was reached by the victorious nations both judges and partakers in this decision. Inaction on the part of the victor nations would have deprived the world of a verdict, the necessity of which was universally felt."[13]

This is the entire passage. What decision "prior to the trial" could Bernard be talking about? Does his final sentence refer to that prior decision or to the verdict of the trial? It is not clear. But at least Bernard himself believed that the issue of responsibility for the war had already been decided before the trial. Even so, held Bernard, that decision did not materially affect the fairness of the Tokyo trial.

Justice Pal placed his trust in the moral integrity of his fellow justices. Wrote Pal: "The judges are here no doubt from the different victor nations, but they are here in their personal capacities. One of the essential factors usually considered in the selection of members of such tribunals is *moral integrity*." He went on to discuss the danger of unconscious bias, but he concluded: ". . . in spite of all such obstacles it is human justice with which the accused must rest content."[14] Like the majority judgment, Pal rejected the defense challenge.

No justice conceded that a trial by the victors of the vanquished was by definition unfair.[15] But in the light of our knowledge about the Tokyo trial, we may question

[13] Bernard, "Dissenting Judgment," pp. 2-3.
[14] Pal, *Judgment*, p. 7.
[15] Wrote Justice Röling twelve years later of the exclusion of neutral and Japanese judges: "This was a grave error." Bert V. A. Röling, "The Tokyo Trial in Retrospect," in Susumu Yamaguchi, ed., *Buddhism and Culture* (Kyoto: Nakano Press, 1960), p. 257.

the implicit confidence of these men in their own impartiality. The uncertain state of international law and the brilliant arguments of Takayanagi and the other defense counsel affected the judgment of only one justice out of eleven. This fact alone seems indicative of a lack of impartiality. (It may not be only coincidence that this single justice was one of three Asian justices, the only one of the three whose country had not suffered directly and severely from Japanese acts in the Pacific war.) As we shall see, the flagrant procedural flaws of the trial affected the judgment of only two justices. And only one justice seriously contested the tribunal's version of recent Japanese history. The appointment of justices only from among the aggrieved and victor nations itself may not invalidate the tribunal's judgment, but it raises serious questions about the tribunal's impartiality.

A second area of challenge concerned the qualifications of individual justices. Would men with prior involvement in the issues to come before the court be disqualified from sitting as justices? One problem was that few men in positions of trust had not been involved in the war in one way or another. To be sure, however, there were types and degrees of involvement. A second problem was the divergence in practice between common law and civil law. In the United States prior knowledge is grounds for disqualification; but this is not so of civil law jurisdictions. These two considerations lie behind the statement at London of the Soviet delegate, General I. T. Nikitchenko: ". . . with regard to the position of the judge the Soviet Delegation considers that there is no necessity in trials of this sort to accept the principle that the judge is a completely disinterested party with no previous knowledge of the case.

[Nikitchenko had just said that the criminals 'have already been convicted.'] The case for the prosecution is undoubtedly known to the judge before the trial starts and there is, therefore, no necessity to create a sort of fiction that the judge is a disinterested person who has no legal knowledge of what has happened before."[16]

But inexplicable from an American point of view is the ease with which the United States acquiesced in the removal of barriers to judicial bias.

The results at Nuremberg were as follows. The Soviet Union appointed as its justice General Nikitchenko himself. The French Government appointed its London representative as alternate justice. The United States appointed as its justice Francis J. Biddle, Attorney General under Franklin D. Roosevelt and a co-author of the memorandum quoted at length in Chapter 1. That memorandum expressed a preference for military justices, such justices ". . . being less likely to give undue weight to technical contentions and legalistic arguments."

At Tokyo there were five justices (of eleven) to whom exception might have been taken for one reason or another. The Chinese justice, Mei Ju-ao, was not a judge in his native land. He was a politician, acting chairman of the foreign affairs committee of the Nationalist legislature.[17] The Russian justice, Major General I. M. Zaryanov, under-

[16] *London Conference*, p. 105.

[17] The Chinese justice, Mei Ju-ao, did have a law degree from the University of Chicago (1928). However he was not a judge in China either before or after the Tokyo trial. Hence, he was unduly subject to political pressure. It may be that he owed his appointment to his friendship with Sun Fo, son of Sun Yat-sen and then president of the Legislative Yuan. James T. C. Liu, letter to author, December 8, 1969.

stood neither English nor Japanese, the two official languages of the trial. During the trial he was assisted by a corps of Russian interpreters (not part of the official language section and presumably unsworn);[18] and interpreters must have accompanied him to all conferences with the other judges.

The Philippine justice, the second American justice, and the Australian justice all had prior involvement in the issues to come before the tribunal. The Philippine justice, Delfin Jaranilla, had been involved most directly: he was a survivor of the infamous Bataan death march and had been a prisoner of war in Japanese hands for the duration of the war.[19] The second American justice, Major General

[18] Horwitz, "Tokyo Trial," p. 488, n. 25. Horwitz seems to balance the Soviet justice's language disability with the Soviet associate prosecutor's facility in English, but of course there is no relation whatsoever between the two. There is also some question as to the language ability of the French justice, Bernard. Several sources suggest he did not understand English. Gordon Ireland, "Uncommon Law in Martial Tokyo," *The Year Book of World Affairs*, 4:59 (1950); editor's note preceding George F. Blewett, "Victor's Injustice: The Tokyo War Crimes Trial," *American Perspective*, 4.3:282 (Summer 1950). A note to the author from Defense Counsel George A. Furness states: "As I remember, our earphones had three switches, one for English, one for Japanese and one for Russian, so that simultaneous interpretation was made into Russian for all testimony. I do not know who interpreted into Russian; probably the Russian prosecution provided for it. I do not know how documents were translated into Russian."

[19] Biographical data supplied to author by Felicitas Peto, Secretary to Justice Jaranilla, Nov. 13, 1969; see also *Proceedings in Chambers*, June 12, 1946, pp. 20-22, for discussion of motion "suggesting the disqualification and personal bias of the Philippine justice of the tribunal." President Webb expresses there his concern over the criterion used by the tribunal to reject the challenge to his own fitness (see text, p. 83). Webb favored leaving the issue of fitness up to the individual justice. There is a strong im-

Myron H. Cramer, had submitted to President Roosevelt a legal brief on the responsibility for the attack on Pearl Harbor.[20] The Australian justice, President Webb, had been Australian war crimes commissioner during the war, and in that role he had investigated Japanese atrocities on New Guinea.[21]

The defense challenged the Australian justice's qualifications at the very start of the trial. To consider this challenge the tribunal recessed and returned after fifteen minutes to announce through the justice from New Zealand: "The members of the tribunal are of opinion that no objection to the person of any member of the tribunal can be sustained."[22] This holding was not a vote of confidence in President Webb. It was instead a decision not to consider *any* objections to *any* member of the tribunal. What reasoning lay behind this decision? The charter bore no provision for such review. His position as justice and president reaffirmed, President Webb commented that he had considered this question himself before accepting appointment and had decided he was eligible to serve.[23]

Except on the issue of his qualification to serve and in his absence, President Webb spoke for the tribunal. A number of observers have contended that President Webb conducted the trial in a manner prejudicial to justice. For example, abuse of defense counsel was a regular feature of the trial. Consider the words of one American specialist

---

plication in Webb's language that the Philippine justice should have disqualified himself.

[20] Owen Cunningham, "Address," American Bar Association, "Proceedings of the Section on International and Comparative Law, Seattle Meeting, September 6-7, 1948," p. 36.

[21] *Proceedings*, pp. 92ff.   [22] *Ibid.*, p. 98.   [23] *Ibid.*, p. 98.

in the field of war crimes trials: "The attitude of the president of the tribunal throughout toward defense counsel was one not consistent with the standards commonly observed in courts of the United States. . . . Arrogance on the part of the court by reason of its exalted position is considered in this country to be a violation of judicial ethics, and an indication of the weakness of the man presiding."[24] One of the defense counsel, speaking to the American Bar Association while the trial was in progress (the speech caused his disqualification from the trial), charged that President Webb displayed a similarly hostile attitude toward defense witnesses. Most noteworthy here was Webb's exasperated outburst during the testimony of Admiral Yonai Mitsumasa, who had served as prime minister during the first half of 1940. Said Webb: "The Prime Minister is the most stupid witness I have ever listened to."[25]

It should be noted that President Webb was also curt on occasion with representatives of the prosecution, notably Chief Prosecutor Keenan. Early in the trial President Webb defended himself against newspaper criticism of his conduct. Said Webb: "There is also reference to my attitude toward defense counsel more particularly. It is said I speak with some asperity and the qualification is made that I do so naturally. Whether that is a compliment or not, I cannot say; but I can assure you that sometimes terse-

[24] Appleman, *Military Tribunals*, pp. 243-244; see also Tsai, "Judicial Administration of the Laws of War," VI, 33.

[25] *Proceedings*, p. 28,939. Cunningham ("Address," p. 35) gives an inaccurate version of the statement. See also Maruyama Masao, *Gendai seiji no shiso to kodo* (Tokyo: Miraisha, 1964), p. 103. Maruyama uses the incident as an illustration of the nebulousness of the thought patterns of Japanese politicians rather than as an example of hostility on President Webb's part.

example, abuse of defense counsel was a regular feature probably I am a bit terse. That is a feature of my country, and perhaps ... terseness may be mistaken for asperity."[26]

* * * * * * * *[27]

All eleven justices shared the disability of being citizens of the victor nations. Five justices were vulnerable to more specific challenge: that they had prior involvement in the issues to come before the tribunal; that they lacked the necessary languages; that they were not judges. All five supported the majority judgment, if not all of the sentences, and the Philippine justice complained that some of the sentences were too lenient.[28] When we consider (see

[26] *Proceedings*, p. 1,288. The author does not feel qualified to assess the issue of judicial etiquette. I must rely instead on the judgments of the three students of international military tribunals who have examined the record of the Tokyo trial. It is significant that the first two are proponents of the basic concept of the Nuremberg and Tokyo trials. Appleman (*Military Tribunals*, pp. 243-244) gives a list of examples of abuse of defense counsel; so also does Paul Chung-tseng Tsai, "Judicial Administration of the Laws of War: Procedures in War Crimes Trials," Doctor of Law thesis (Yale, 1957), F/VI/18, n. 172. See also Gordon Ireland, "Uncommon Law in Martial Tokyo," p. 66. Woetzel (*The Nuremberg Trials in International Law*) deals with Tokyo only very briefly.

[27] The first two printings of this book carried a paragraph here charging President Webb with "blatant" prejudice. I attributed to President Webb a statement from the *Proceedings* (p. 1,648) that the Pacific War "should not have been begun and . . . cannot be defended." Re-examination of the *Proceedings* discloses that the speaker was a member of the prosecution. I offer my apology to President Webb.

[28] Jaranilla, "Concurring Opinion," p. 34.

below) that the majority consisted of six, seven, or at most nine justices, we see how important was the role played by these five men.

We have discussed factors that disqualified all or some of the justices. What of positive qualifications? How many of the men appointed to this international military tribunal had any background in international law? The answer is one: Justice Pal.[29]

2. The Rules By Which the Justices Operated

The Nuremberg bench consisted of four justices, a not unwieldy number. Each justice had an alternate. A justice could be replaced during the trial "for reasons of health or for other good reasons," but only by his alternate. Because of the large size of the bench at Tokyo, no alternate justices were appointed; yet no provision was made for the replacement of justices. Since the trial lasted over two and one half years, it was to be expected that there should be vacancies on the bench. The remarkable thing is that only two vacancies occurred.

The original French justice was replaced by a second appointee even before the trial began; the second French appointee was present throughout the trial.[30] The original American justice, John P. Higgins, Chief Justice of the Superior Court of Massachusetts, resigned in July 1946,

[29] Takayanagi Kenzo, "Some Reflections on the Future of War Crimes," Appendix to Appeal of Defendant Suzuki, p. 4, in "Proceedings on Review Before General MacArthur." Takayanagi argued that the Tokyo bench included no one "known to the profession of international law, with the solitary exception of Justice Pal of India, who is a member of the International Law Association."

[30] *Judgment*, p. 7.

86

three months after his appointment and one month after the tribunal had begun to hear evidence. Justice Higgins expressed his fear that the trial would last into 1947 (it ended in November 1948) and his desire to return to judicial tasks at home.[31] His departure hardly bespoke great respect for the judicial task at Tokyo. Higgins was replaced by Major General Myron H. Cramer, Judge Advocate General of the U.S. Army.

General Cramer's appointment was challenged by the defense on three points: that the charter contained no provision for additional appointments beyond the original eleven justices; that General Cramer could not be familiar with the record of the trial (some 2,300 pages of testimony had been completed); and that he had been an important figure in America's war effort. The tribunal held that these challenges failed; but the president was careful to record that the tribunal's decision had been a majority decision.[32] With General Cramer's appointment, the United States joined the Soviet Union in being represented on the tribunal bench by a military man.

At the insistence of the Russian delegate at the London Conference, the Nuremberg Charter defined a quorum to be the whole panel of four judges or their alternates.[33] By general consent at London, majority rule was invoked, with the president's vote decisive in case of tie. However, convictions and sentences required the affirmative vote of at least three of the four justices.[34]

The Tokyo Charter prescribed somewhat looser procedures. A simple majority (six justices) could convene the

[31] *New York Times*, June 21, 1946; June 26, 1946.
[32] *Proceedings*, pp. 2,342, 2,361.
[33] *London Conference*, p. 234; Nuremberg Charter, Article 4a.
[34] Nuremberg Charter, Article 4c.

tribunal.[35] Five justices could be absent and the trial still proceed. Indeed, the proceedings opened on May 3 with only nine justices present. Justice Pal arrived on May 17 but took no part that day in the rejection of all the preliminary motions filed by the defense.[36] The Philippine justice arrived on June 9; evidence had been heard since June 3.[37] Judge Cramer arrived on July 22.

Three justices arrived after the trial had begun; but then no justice was required to hear all the testimony. Absences were permitted, and the Tokyo Charter left it up to the individual justice to decide whether his absence disqualified him from further participation in the trial.[38] No justice exercised that option. Some justices had exemplary records of attendance. Justice Cramer of the United States, for example, made up for his absence during the first three months by missing thereafter only one full day and parts of three others. Other justices were not so sedulous. Justice Pal, for example, was absent for more than 80 days of the 417 days upon which the tribunal held sessions. Consider the situation following the June-July recess of 1947. Testimony for the defense resumed when the recess ended on August 4, but only seven justices were present. The Chinese justice reappeared the next day. The British justice, apparently in failing health, returned a week later, on August 11; he had also missed the six days of testimony that preceded the recess. The Canadian justice returned on August 21. The Russian justice returned on September 3. In spite of empty seats on the bench, the trial went on.

On November 7, 1947 President Webb announced that he would return to Australia at the appeal of his Prime

---

[35] Tokyo Charter, Article 4a.   [36] *Proceedings*, p. 318.
[37] *Proceedings*, p. 490.   [38] Article 4c.

The courtroom: justices on right, defendants on left, prosecution and defense counsel in center. In the rear is the gallery for press and visitors.

The courtroom: justices on left, defendants on right. In the rear is a gallery for distinguished visitors.

The justices pose on opening day. Front (l-r): Justices Patrick (G.B.), Higgins (U.S.), Webb (Australia), Mei (China), Zaryanov (U.S.S.R.). Back (l-r): Justices McDougall (Canada), Röling (Netherlands), Bernard (France), Northcroft (New Zealand). Still to arrive are Justices Jaranilla (Philippines) and Pal (India).

Major General Cramer, the second American justice, confers with President Webb.

The bench listens to testimony (l-r): Justices Pal, Röling, McDougall, Patrick, Cramer, Webb, Mei, Zaryanov, Bernard, Northcroft. Justice Jaranilla is out of the picture on the right.

Justice Radhabinod Pal.

President Webb and Justice Mei confer.

The defendants stand as the justices enter the courtroom.

The defendants look on. This partial view of the dock on opening day includes Tojo (left) and Okawa (rear, being restrained by M.P.).

Defendant Shimada testifies.

Defendant Tojo testifies.

Defense counsel Takayanagi Kenzo addresses the court.

Defendant Muto confers with defense counsel.

Chief of Counsel Joseph B. Keenan prepares his case.

Defendant Tojo's American and Japanese counsel confer.

M.P. guard watches as defendants lunch from GI trays (l-r): Hirota, Togo, Tojo, Sato.

The defendants prepare to enter the War Ministry building after arriving from prison by bus.

Minister to take part in the November session of the Australian High Court (in his absence that court had experienced difficulty in mustering a quorum). Webb's absence from the Tokyo trial lasted from November 12 through December 12; he missed twenty-two consecutive days of the trial. Little wonder, then, that Defense Counsel Cunningham, the most outspoken of the lawyers for the defense, should exclaim: "The privilege of absence has been so abused during this trial that it is necessary at this time [Webb's announcement of his absence] that the record show a protest."[39]

A majority constituted a quorum, and the majority vote of those justices present was sufficient to make all decisions and judgments, including verdicts and sentences. In case of tie, the president's vote was decisive.[40] In theory, then, three members of the court, if they included the president and if five members were absent, could make judgments binding on the eleven-member tribunal. (And even with the full court sitting, should the American justice side with the five justices from the British Commonwealth, then Anglo-American legal ideas or political intentions would dominate the panel.)

That these regulations had an important bearing on the judgment, there can be little doubt. By the time of the judgment, the justices had already split into a "majority" of seven and four individual dissenters; the justices from Australia, France, India, and the Netherlands. The 1,050 pages of the judgment relating to findings of fact were drawn up first by a drafting committee, submitted then to the majority, and then distributed to the remaining four justices. As the French justice indicated in his dissent: "...

---

[39] *Proceedings*, p. 32,662.   [40] Article 4b.

the eleven judges were never called to meet to discuss orally a part of or in its entirety this part of the judgments."[41] The French justice considered ". . . oral deliberations outside of all influence bearing on all produced evidence among all the judges who sat at the trials" to be a guarantee of justice, and hence he argued that the verdict was invalid.[42]

In their plea to the Supreme Commander, General MacArthur, after the tribunal had handed down its judgment, the defense counsel stressed these procedural flaws. Their appeal included these words:

"The verdict is not that of the tribunal, but of a clique of it. It has been disclosed that the seven-judge majority excluded from the deliberations and decision not only Messrs. Justices Pal and Bernard, who dissented generally, but Mr. Justice Röling who dissented in part and concurred in part, and the President, Sir William Webb, who expressed grave doubts concerning several points of the result, but recorded no dissent. It is known that death sentences were imposed by vote of six to five in some cases, of seven to four in others, but in no case by vote of more than seven judges. The law of most of the civilized world requires unanimity for imposing a sentence of death, and usually for conviction of a crime; we Americans would consider it an outrage that six or seven men out of eleven

[41] Bernard, "Dissenting Judgment," p. 19.

[42] *Ibid.* Writing in 1960 Justice Röling of the Netherlands commented as follows on this issue: ". . . considerable difference of opinion existed among the Tokyo judges. The dissenting opinion of the French judge Bernard partly discloses the consequences these conflicting opinions had with regard to the cooperation of the judges in chambers." Röling, "Tokyo Trial in Retrospect," p. 258.

should convict and sentence to death, and the community of civilized nations must regard it as an outrage here."[43]

This allegation does seem incredible. Death sentences handed down by one-vote majorities? Preposterous! Considering the composition of the panel of justices, we would not expect a close vote on any of the verdicts or sentences. Yet that seems to have been the case. One of the justices disclosed later—but still before the sentences were carried out—that the vote on Hirota's death penalty had been 6 to 5. On the other six death penalties it had been 7 to 4. In addition, there had been five votes in favor of death sentences for four more of the accused. A simple majority, 6 votes to 5, determined the manner of death: not execution before a firing squad, presumably too dignified a death, but death by hanging.[44]

At Nuremberg, with its four justices, verdicts and sentences required the approval of three justices. Had the rules of operation at Tokyo been only slightly stricter, had

[43] See Appendix 4.

[44] AP despatch, Dec. 8, 1948; *New York Times*, Dec. 9, 1948. The justice did not permit his name to be used. However, he was later identified as Justice Röling. Tateno Nobuyuki, *Zoku Nihon senryo* (Tokyo: Kodansha, 1964), p. 221. Kojima Noboru has speculated that the votes in favor of the death sentences came from the following justices: American, British, Chinese, Filipino, New Zealand, Canadian, and Dutch (who approved all but Hirota's sentence). Four defendants escaped the death penalty by only one vote. According to Kojima's analysis this means that the justices from China, England, New Zealand, and the Philippines voted for 11 death sentences; from the United States, for 9; from Canada, for 8; and from Holland for 7. Webb of Australia, Bernard of France, and Pal of India are on record in opposition to any death sentences; and Kojima speculates that the Soviet judge joined them in opposing death sentences. Kojima, *Tokyo saiban*, II, 191-193.

seven or eight votes been necessary for the verdicts and sentences, the Tokyo trial might have had a very different ending.

The trial of Lieutenant William Calley is fresh in American minds. That court-martial was carried out according to the *Uniform Code of Military Justice.* The *Uniform Code* dates back to a Congressional enactment of May 5, 1950. Amendments have been made since 1950, but none has affected the regulations which follow. Article 52b reads as follows:

"(1) No person may be sentenced to suffer death, except by the concurrence of all the members of the court-martial present at the time the vote is taken. . . .

"(2) No person may be sentenced to life imprisonment or to confinement for more than ten years, except by the concurrence of three-fourths of the members present at the time the vote is taken. [Fractions are to be rounded off upward.]

"(3) All other sentences shall be determined by the concurrence of two-thirds of the members present at the time the vote is taken."

Despite these tight rules, Lieutenant Calley was found guilty and sentenced to life imprisonment—at least, he was so sentenced before President Nixon intervened dramatically.

Had *these* procedures been in force in Tokyo, there could have been no death sentences. Nine votes would have been necessary for sentences over ten years, and eight votes for lesser sentences. Justices Bernard and Pal were in strong dissent, so nine votes was the highest count the majority could muster. However, Justice Röling dissented on five convictions. Hence, there could have been no more than twenty life sentences and five sentences of less than ten years. As it was, there were seven death sentences, sixteen life sentences, one twenty-year sentence, and one seven-year sentence.

3. The Selection of the Accused

Two facets of the selection of the accused at Tokyo merit attention. First, all individuals accused at Tokyo were Japanese, and the acts with which they were charged had been committed in the defeated cause of Japan. Second, the selection of which Japanese citizens should stand trial was arbitrary at best. Let us consider each of these points in turn.

JAPANESE ONLY

Just as the justices at Tokyo came only from the aggrieved and victor nations, so the accused were all Japanese. Were war crimes in the Pacific war the exclusive preserve of the Japanese enemy? At the London Conference the Russians and the French had urged that any definition of criminal acts specify acts committed by the European Axis powers. In General Nikitchenko's words, this meant that "... a person who had not acted on the part of the European Axis powers would not have committed a crime."[45] Robert H. Jackson objected strongly to any such formulation, with the result that acts were defined without respect to the actor. However, the first part of the relevant article of the Nuremberg Charter did specify that the Nuremberg Tribunal was empowered to try only enemy acts: "The tribunal established by the Agreement ... for the trial and punishment of the major war criminals

[45] *London Conference*, p. 387.

93

of the European Axis countries shall have the power to try and punish persons who, acting in the interests of the European Axis countries . . . committed any of the following crimes."[46] The Tokyo Charter made no such limitation. It called for the punishment of "major war criminals in the Far East" (Art. 1) and "Far Eastern War Criminals" (Art. 5). Nowhere in the charter did the words "Japan" or "Far Eastern Axis" appear. Nevertheless, the indictment concerned Japanese acts only.

The fact that other criminals go unpunished is not a valid defense in domestic law. In the case of the Tokyo trial and international law, however, two considerations greatly increase the cogency of this objection. In domestic law, crimes are well defined; but at Tokyo crimes were not well defined. In the words of Justice Pal: "It may be suggested . . . that simply because there might be robbers untried and unpunished it would not follow that robbing is no crime and a robber placed under trial for robbery would gain nothing by showing that there are other robbers in the world who are going unpunished. This is certainly sound logic when we know for certain that robbery is a crime. When, however, we are still to determine whether or not a particular act in a particular community is or is not criminal, I believe it is a pertinent enquiry how the act in question stands in relation to the other members of the community and how the community looks upon the act when done by such other members."[47] Hence the importance of defining such terms as "aggression." Second, the issue was not simply that other "criminals" were going unpunished; it was that other "criminals" were sitting in judgment on Japanese "criminals."

There can be no doubt that the victor nations in the

[46] Nuremberg Charter, Article 6.　　[47] Pal, *Judgment*, p. 118.

Pacific war committed many of the acts for which the Japanese stood indicted at Tokyo. For our present purposes it will suffice to consider two such acts: the Soviet Union's declaration of war on Japan; and the American dropping of the atomic bombs.

(A.) The Soviet Union's Declaration of War Against Japan

In the final days of the Pacific war, on August 8, 1945, the Soviet Union declared war on Japan. At that time Japan stood on the brink of total military defeat. Her last island bastion, Okinawa, had fallen in June. Since July the American navy had paraded up and down Japan's coastline virtually unchallenged. On August 6, the first atomic bomb had been dropped on Hiroshima. Indeed, as early as July 13, Japan had sought the mediation of the Soviet Union to end the war. That Japan turned to the Soviet Union was due in part to the existence of a neutrality pact between the two nations. This pact, signed on April 13, 1941, was in effect throughout the war. By April 1945 the Soviet Union had notified the Japanese Government that it did not wish to renew the pact beyond its expiration date, but that expiration date was April 1946.[48]

Why, then, did the Soviet Union declare war? Its own declaration read in part: "After the defeat and capitulation of Hitlerite Germany, Japan remained the only great power which still stands for the continuation of the war. . . . Taking into account the refusal of Japan to capitulate, the Allies approached the Soviet Government with a proposal to join the war against Japanese aggression and thus shorten the duration of the war, reduce the number of casualties, and contribute toward the most speedy restora-

[48] Butow, *Japan's Decision*, pp. 58-59.

95

tion of peace. True to its obligation as an ally, the Soviet Government has accepted the proposal of the Allies. . . . The Soviet Government considers that this policy is the only means able to bring peace nearer, to free the people from further sacrifice and suffering, and to give the Japanese people the opportunity of avoiding the danger of destruction suffered by Germany after her refusal to accept unconditional surrender."[49] The justification offered was not one of self-defense; rather it was one of policy, of ending the war quickly.

As the Soviet declaration indicated, the Allies had actively solicited the Soviet entry into the Pacific war. At Yalta and at Potsdam, American civilian and military leaders had looked hopefully to an early Soviet involvement in Manchuria as a way of reducing our own casualties.[50] At Potsdam the Soviet Union had asked for a formal request to that end from the Allies. In the words of Secretary of State James F. Byrnes: "The Soviet Government, Molotov said, considered that the best method would be for the United States, Great Britain, and the other Allies to address a formal request to the Soviet Government for its entry into the war." Byrnes continued: "The request presented a problem to us. The Soviet Union had a non-aggression pact with the Japanese. The Soviet Government also had had a similar pact with Hitler, but it was the Nazis who had violated that one. We did not believe the United States Government should be placed in the position of asking another government to violate its agreement without good and sufficient reason. The Soviet

[49] Text in *ibid.*, pp. 153-154.

[50] Edward R. Stettinius, Jr., *Roosevelt and the Russians: The Yalta Conference*, ed. Walter Johnson (Garden City: Doubleday, 1949), p. 98; quoted in Butow, *Japan's Decision*, p. 154, n. 44.

Union had notified Japan a few months earlier of its intention to abrogate the treaty but it would still be in force for nearly a year. The President was disturbed."[51]

"Without good and sufficient reason"—that was the important phrase. It took an hour or two, but Secretary Byrnes did come up with two pretexts: the Moscow Declaration of October 30, 1943, and the wording of two articles (103 and 106) of the *proposed* United Nations Charter. Article 103 stated that ". . . in the event of a conflict between the obligations of the Members of the United Nations under the present charter and their obligations under any other international agreement, their obligations under the present charter shall prevail."[52] The letter by which President Truman solicited the intervention of the Soviet Union concluded: "Though the charter has not been formally ratified, at San Francisco, it was agreed to by the Representative of the Soviet Socialist Republics and the Soviet Government will be one of the permanent members of the Security Council. It seems to me that under the terms of the Moscow Declaration and the provisions of the charter . . . it would be proper for the Soviet Union to indicate its willingness to consult and cooperate with other great powers now at war with Japan with a view to joint action on behalf of the community of nations to maintain peace and security."[53]

Thus, the American Government provided the Soviet Government a flimsy justification for the unilateral abrogation of an existing treaty in favor of a treaty not yet ratified. Wrote Secretary Byrnes: "The President later told me that Generalissimo Stalin expressed great appreciation

---

[51] James F. Byrnes, *Speaking Frankly* (New York: Harper and Brothers, 1947), pp. 207-208.

[52] Quoted in *ibid.*, p. 208.   [53] Quoted in *ibid.*, pp. 208-209.

of the communication. He should have. The Soviet Government's statement announcing its entry into the war did not include a reference to Section 103 of the Charter, but our finding it for Mr. Molotov will enable the Soviet historian to show that Russia's declaration of war on Japan was in accordance with what they like to claim is their scrupulous regard for international obligations."[54]

At Nuremberg and at Tokyo the Allies invoked the Pact of Paris as the sole criterion in terms of which German and Japanese military activity was illegal and thus criminal. The Pact of Paris (Article 1) stated: "The High Contracting Parties solemnly declare in the names of their respective peoples that they condemn recourse to war for the solution of international controversies and renounce it as an instrument of national policy in their relations to one another."[55] Granted even the large sphere reserved for self-defense by the signatories to the pact, the attack of the Soviet Union could not be construed as self-defense. Not even the Soviet Union itself sought to do that. In this situation the definition of aggression offered by Robert H. Jackson at the London Conference assumes major importance. That definition read in part: "No political, military, economic, or other considerations shall serve as an excuse or justification for such actions; but exercise of the right of legitimate self-defense, that is, resistance to an act of aggression, or action to assist a state which has been subjected to aggression, shall not constitute a war of aggression."[56]

Not even Jackson himself suggested that this second clause was a part of the Pact of Paris, but for the Allies it was surely convenient. It justified the actions of the United

---

[54] *Ibid.*, p. 209.   [55] Quoted in *Nuremberg Judgment*, I, 220.
[56] *London Conference*, p. 294.

States in moving away from neutrality in 1940 and 1941; it exonerated the Soviet attack on Japan in August 1945; and it exonerated also the American complicity in that attack. One definition for the Allies (the Jackson definition); one for the enemy (the Pact of Paris). Such actions may be good politics; but they are bad justice. Either all are guilty, or none. As Justice Pal wrote: "In my opinion we should not put such a construction on the pact which would lead us to hold that all these big powers [the U.S.S.R., the U.S., and the Netherlands[57]] participated in a criminal act."[58]

(B.) The American Dropping of the Atomic Bombs

By the standard of the Pact of Paris—at least as construed by the Nuremberg judgment and the majority judgment at Tokyo—the Soviet Union was guilty of the "crime against peace." Similarly, the United States had come under grave suspicion of guilt for a "crime against humanity." The Tokyo Charter defined that crime as ". . . inhumane acts against any civilian population."[59] Did this definition not apply to the atomic bombing of Hiroshima and Nagasaki?

Consider the setting. Japan was prostrate. The American Government knew that Japan had asked the Soviet Union to mediate an end to the war. There could be no plea of military necessity. Nor in that long-distant day before Vietnam could military necessity justify wholesale slaughter of civilians. There could be only the argument that the

[57] The Netherlands had declared war on Japan on December 8, 1941, more than a month before Japan declared war on the Netherlands and attacked the Dutch East Indies.

[58] Pal, *Judgment*, p. 117.

[59] Nuremberg Charter, Article 6c; Tokyo Charter, Article 5c.

99

atomic bombs had shortened the war and saved American lives. But the Tokyo Charter did not provide for such exoneration in the case of Japanese war crimes.

The Tokyo tribunal held that evidence concerning the dropping of the atomic bombs was inadmissible, and the majority judgment did not mention the issue; but three justices did. In his "Concurring Opinion," Justice Jaranilla of the Philippines endorsed the dropping of the bombs in these terms: "If a means is justified by an end, the use of the atomic bomb was justified."[60] In his dissent Justice Pal alluded to German actions in World War I. He wrote: "The Kaiser Wilhelm II was credited with a letter to the Austrian Kaiser Franz Joseph in the early days of that war [World War I], wherein he stated as follows: 'My soul is torn, but everything must be put to fire and sword; men, women and children, and old men must be slaughtered and not a tree or house be left standing. With these methods of terrorism, which are alone capable of affecting a people as degenerate as the French, the war will be over in two months, whereas if I admit considerations of humanity it will be prolonged for years. In spite of my repugnance I have therefore been obliged to choose the former system.' This showed his ruthless policy, and this policy of indiscriminate murder to shorten the war was considered to be a crime." Justice Pal continued: "In the Pacific war under our consideration, if there was anything approaching what is indicated in the above letter of the German Emperor, it is the decision coming from the Allied Powers to use the atom bomb. . . . If any indiscriminate destruction of civilian life and property is still illegitimate in warfare, then, in the Pacific war, this decision to

[60] Jaranilla, "Concurring Opinion," p. 25.

use the atom bomb is the only near approach to the directives of the German Emperor during the first world war and of the Nazi leaders during the second world war. Nothing like this could be traced to the credit of the present accused."[61] Writing twelve years after the end of the Tokyo trial Justice Röling of the Netherlands commented: ". . . from the Second World War above all two things are remembered: the German gas chambers and the American atomic bombings."[62]

[61] Pal, *Judgment*, pp. 620-621.

[62] Röling, "Tokyo Trial in Retrospect," p. 248. The Shimoda case in Japan (decided on Dec. 7, 1963 in the District Court of Tokyo) involved an assertion that the atomic bombings were illegal acts. In this, the only court judgment on the issue, the District Court held unanimously that the bombings were "illegal by positive international law at that time." For the decision, see *Japan Annual of International Law* (1954), pp. 212-252; the decision is analyzed in Richard N. Falk, "Shimoda Case: A Legal Appraisal of the Atomic Attacks on Hiroshima and Nagasaki," *American Journal of International Law*, 59:759-793 (October 1965). For one presentation of the argument that the bombings were "illegal by positive international law at that time," see the brief submitted in the Shimoda Case by Tabata Shigejiro. I am indebted to Professor Tabata for showing me this brief.

Noteworthy in this connection is the comment by Brigadier General Telford Taylor, an important figure in the Nuremberg prosecutions: "The rights and wrongs of Hiroshima are debatable, but I have never heard a plausible justification of Nagasaki. It is difficult to contest the judgment that Dresden and Nagasaki were war crimes, tolerable in retrospect only because their malignancy pales in comparison to Dachau, Auschwitz, and Treblinka" (*Nuremberg and Vietnam: An American Tragedy* [Chicago: Quadrangle, 1970], p. 143). Dachau, Auschwitz, and Treblinka may bear on our judgment of Dresden; but what is to be set in the scales to offset Nagasaki? The ghost of the Axis Alliance (see below, pages 140-144) lives on in Taylor's thinking: German atrocities seem somehow to offset our war crimes against Japan.

Nevertheless, the Soviet declaration of war on Japan and the American atomic bombings were not included in the indictment at the Tokyo trial; and the American and Russian justices voted with the majority to convict the Japanese leaders of conspiracy to wage aggressive war, of waging aggressive war, and of ordering, authorizing, and permitting the commission of conventional war crimes.

WHICH JAPANESE?

Only Japanese stood accused at Tokyo. It remains to ask: which Japanese? Consider first the words of Chief Prosecutor Keenan in his Opening Statement: "Among its other duties, the prosecution has had the particularly heavy task of selecting from the large number of persons who might properly have been charged in this indictment those whose responsibility for the crimes set forth in the charter appeared from the available evidence to be the greatest. In order that these proceedings would not become impossibly unwieldy, it was necessary to limit the number of the accused in the indictment now before this tribunal. . . . It may well be that if all the facts were now known to us, there are persons not now on trial whom we might have charged in preference to some of the accused."[63] In fact, some 260 high Japanese officials were in Allied custody before the Tokyo trial began.[64] From these 260 the prosecution had made its selection.

[63] "Trial of Japanese War Criminals," p. 35.

[64] Robert J. C. Butow, *Tojo and the Coming of the War* (Princeton: Princeton University Press, 1961), p. 445, lists 40 suspects arrested in September 1945. E. J. Lewe van Aduard, *Japan: From Surrender to Peace* (New York: Praeger, 1954), p. 30, lists an additional 222 arrests between November 19, 1945, and January 15, 1946.

Solis Horwitz, one of the prosecution lawyers at Tokyo and author of a valuable report on the trial, has described the selection process. He writes: "Many long sessions of the Executive Committee [for the prosecution, consisting of all Associate Counsel and 'several senior members of the United States staff'] were devoted to the problem of the choice of defendants. The final selection was the result of an arduous process of weighing and balancing the guilt of one suspect against that of another. In cases where the Committee was not unanimous either for inclusion or for exclusion, other attorneys were asked to review the matter and prepare new dossiers. In cases of highly controversial figures the attorneys who had prepared the dossiers appeared before the Committee to elaborate their views and were closely questioned on their recommendations."

Horwitz went on to specify the criteria for selection: that the accused could be charged with committing crimes against peace; that the group of accused be representative of the various branches of the Japanese Government and of the various phases of the period covered by the indictment; that the accused be the "principal leaders" with "primary responsibility for the acts committed"; and that there be an overwhelming case against each accused. In Horwitz' words: "No person was to be included as a defendant unless the evidence against him was so strong as to render negligible the chances for acquittal."[65] Working with these criteria the Executive Committee took ten weeks to reduce 260 to 26, a number larger than originally planned.[66]

[65] Horwitz, "Tokyo Trial," 495-496.
[66] *Ibid.*, p. 496. Writes Horwitz: "The Committee had hoped to limit the number of defendants for the first trial (which eventually

103

Seventeen of the twenty-six selected for trial were military men.[67] Three were navy men, all of the rank of admiral. Two had served as navy minister, and all had played important roles in planning between 1940 and 1944. Fourteen were army officers, and they were a much more heterogeneous group. One was a mere colonel; his primary accomplishments had been in the realm of propaganda and intrigue. One was a general who had resigned in 1938; before that time military attaché in Berlin, he served thereafter for five years as ambassador to Nazi Germany. One general had held no important posts outside the army.

---

became the first and only trial) to fifteen, but the length of the period involved and the number of important events made it impossible to select a representative group of less than twenty-eight. Even this list excluded many of the principal leaders of the aggressive policy who either had died or had grown so old as to raise serious doubts whether they would survive a trial of considerable duration. Had these other leaders been available, there is no doubt that they would have replaced in the dock some of the defendants finally chosen."

[67] I have based this account and the analysis that follows on Horwitz' account. Horwitz leaves the impression that the Executive Committee reduced the 260 to twenty-six, and that the final number of twenty-eight was reached when the Soviet Union urged the addition of Shigemitsu and Umezu (see below, pp. 107-109). However, Horwitz is not explicit; nor when he is explicit is he entirely reliable. Kojima (*Tokyo saiban*, I, 111) offers a different version. By his account the Executive Committee reduced the 260 to twenty-eight. The twenty-eight included the twenty-six persons presently under discussion, plus two others: former prime minister General Abe Nobuyuki and General Mazaki Jinzaburo, an important figure in the army intrigues of the early 1930's. Shigemitsu Mamoru reported hearing a similar account from Tanaka Ryukichi. *Sugamo nikki* (Tokyo: Bunshun shinsha, 1953), p. 205. See below, note 70. The inclusion of Abe and Mazaki would alter somewhat the figures that follow. For brief biographical information on the defendants, see Appendix 3.

104

Eight generals had held cabinet posts: one had been Minister without Portfolio in the Tojo cabinet, and seven had been Army Minister. Every army minister from June 1938 to July 1944 was included. Of these seven, one had served also as Minister of Education from May 1938 to August 1939 (in which capacity, the Judgment would read, he "approved and collaborated in military operations in . . . China");[68] and two had served as Prime Minister. Of the whole group of seventeen military men, eleven had been members at various times of the Supreme War Council, and nine had held wartime (1937-1945) commands.

Nine of the twenty-six were civilians. One had never held any high governmental post; like the army colonel, he had been a propagandist. Four were career foreign service officers.[69] Three of these men had served as Foreign Minister, and one—Hirota—had become Prime Minister. One other civilian had served as Prime Minister (making four prime ministers in all), one had served primarily in the Imperial Household, and two had served in posts connected with economic planning and development at home and abroad.

Four prime ministers stood accused. Assuming that Prime Minister Konoe would have been indicted had he lived (he committed suicide upon learning that an order for his arrest had been issued), every prime minister from June 1937 to the end of the war stood accused, with three exceptions: Abe (August 1939 to January 1940), Yonai (January 1940 to July 1940), and Suzuki (April 1945 to

[68] *Judgment*, p. 1,147.
[69] Miwa Kai and Philip B. Yampolsky, *Political Chronology of Japan, 1885-1957* (New York: Columbia East Asian Institute Studies No. 5, 1957) is a handy reference for cabinet-level positions.

August 1945). Three foreign ministers stood accused, but not the men who held that office in these years: April 1936 to June 1937, May 1938 to July 1940, July 1941 to October 1941, September 1942 to August 1945. One cabinet (Hayashi, February 1937 to June 1937) was not represented at all. Five cabinets, including the Abe cabinet (August 1939 to January 1940) and the Koiso cabinet (July 1944 to April 1945) were represented by only one man.

Four cabinets were represented by five or more ministers. The Tojo cabinet (October 1941 to July 1944) was one of these. Of twenty-seven ministers, five had been chosen. They included the Prime Minister, one Foreign Minister, one Finance Minister, the Navy Minister (Tojo himself was Army Minister), and one Minister without Portfolio. Several absences were noteworthy. The cabinet's second and third foreign ministers were not included; they had held that office for twenty-two of the thirty-three months the cabinet lasted. Missing were six of seven ministers without portfolio. Missing also were the Minister for Greater East Asia and the Minister for Education. The Minister for Education held that office from June 1940 to April 1943, and we have seen that the majority judgment would find one of his predecessors in that office guilty of collaboration in the years 1938 and 1939.

The absence most celebrated in later years was that of the man who had served for the full duration of the Tojo Cabinet, first for two years as Minister of Commerce and Industry and then for nine months as Minister without Portfolio. This man, Kishi Nobusuke, would serve in postwar cabinets as Foreign Minister and as Prime Minister. It was with Kishi in 1960 that the United States would negotiate the renewal until 1970 of the Mutual Security

Pact. The riots surrounding the renewal of the pact, Japan's most spectacular postwar riots, would cost President Eisenhower his planned trip to Japan and Prime Minister Kishi his office.

Consider two other absences. Admiral Yonai Mitsumasa served in six cabinets between 1937 and the surrender. He was Navy Minister from February 1937 to August 1939 and from July 1944 to the surrender. He was Prime Minister from January 1940 to July 1940 and Deputy Premier from July 1944 to April 1945. Arita Hachiro was Foreign Minister in four cabinets between March 1936 and July 1940, serving twenty-seven of those fifty-two months. Neither of these two men stood accused, yet on the surface their involvement would appear far more significant than that, for example, of the three civilians who had never held cabinet positions.

Thus, after winnowing the dossiers of the 260 prime suspects, the Executive Committee settled on twenty-six men ranging from an ambassador to foreign ministers, from a civilian without official position to ministers without portfolio to prime ministers, from a colonel without wartime command to service ministers to wartime chiefs of staff. All the accused on whom judgment would be passed (two died, one was held unfit for trial) would be found guilty of conspiracy, of aggression, of conventional war crimes, or of some combination of the three.

But the story of the selection process does not end here, for the Executive Committee had made its decisions without the advice of the Soviet Union. The Associate Counsel for the Soviet Union, its representative on the Executive Committee, arrived in Tokyo late in April, 1946, ". . . only a few days before the indictment was scheduled to be

107

lodged with the Tribunal." Fortunately for the Executive Committee, the Soviet representative approved the selections already made by the committee. However, to quote Horwitz' account, the newcomer ". . . requested that the defendants Shigemitsu and Umezu, who had not previously been considered as principal offenders, be added and this was done upon his assurance that there was sufficient evidence to establish their guilt."[70] Under pressure of time and in the interest of pleasing the Soviet Union, the Executive Committee suspended its own "arduous process" of decision and agreed to indict two men simply because the Russian Associate Counsel gave his "assurance" that the men could be convicted.

Shigemitsu Mamoru, a career diplomat, had served in many posts: Minister to China, Ambassador to the Soviet Union, Ambassador to Great Britain, Ambassador to Nanking, Vice-Foreign Minister (1933-1936), and Foreign Minister (April 1943 to July 1944) in the Tojo cabinet. Umezu Yoshijiro, a general, had also held a long list of high positions, including Commander of the Japanese forces in China (1934), Vice-War Minister (1936-1938), Commander of the Kwantung Army and Ambassador to Manchukuo (1939-1944), and Chief of the General Staff (July 1944-1945). Thus, there existed a strong prima facie case against each man, but both had been passed over by the Executive Committee. What motive did the Soviet

[70] Horwitz, "Tokyo Trial," p. 496. Kojima's account (see above, note 68) indicates that the inclusion of Shigemitsu and Umezu meant the dropping of Abe and Mazaki from the list of defendants, and that Keenan and MacArthur consented only under the threat of a Soviet walkout. The arrest of Shigemitsu took place on April 29, the very day the indictment was lodged with the tribunal. Kojima, *Tokyo saiban*, I, 109-113.

Union have in forcing their indictment? It is tempting to speculate that the involvement of these two men with Japan's posture toward the Soviet Union—Shigemitsu as ambassador (1936-1938), Umezu as commander of the Kwantung Army (1936-1944) on the Soviet Union's East Asian frontier—brought down upon them the wrath of the Soviet Union.[71] Problems like this must have been behind one remarkable passage in Chief Prosecutor Keenan's Opening Statement. Keenan spoke of the complexities of preparing an indictment ". . . against a large number of individuals who are accused of numerous offenses within the tribunal's jurisdiction, where the prosecution is composed of eleven great peoples each having its national interests and policies to consider. . . . It is necessary to express the views of each nation. . . ."[72]

The tribunal would find Shigemitsu innocent of conspiracy but guilty on six counts of aggression—not planning aggressive war or initiating aggressive war, but waging aggressive war—and one count of "reckless disregard of legal duty" to prevent war crimes; he would get the shortest sentence of all, seven years. The tribunal would find Umezu guilty of the conspiracy and of four counts of aggression; he would get life imprisonment. If the tribunal dealt in this fashion with men whom the prosecution originally omitted from the indictment, then it stands to reason that many other high officials escaped severe punishment only because of the discretion exercised by the Executive Committee.

[71] Shigemitsu's defense counsel feels that Shigemitsu had incurred Russian displeasure for his handling of the Lake Khassan incident.

[72] Keenan, Opening Statement, "Trial of the Japanese War Criminals," p. 8.

Although two men under indictment had served in posts connected with economic planning in North China and Manchuria (one had been Tojo's Minister of Finance), the indictment included no industrialist. According to Horwitz, the Executive Committee sought to distinguish between the industrialist who "for patriotic and economic reasons fills government orders" and the industrialist who "for economic reasons, or otherwise, aids, abets, or collaborates with military and governmental leaders in the formulation and execution of a program of aggression." Horwitz reported: "No evidence was produced to the satisfaction of the Executive Committee that any industrialist occupied the position of a principal formulator of policy." But there was a further consideration. In Horwitz' words: "Conditions in Japan made it important that the indictment of an industrialist not be undertaken unless his conviction was almost a certainty since an acquittal might well have been regarded as a blanket approval of all Japanese industry and industrialists."[73] What is perhaps most remarkable is that the Soviet Union did not insist on the indictment of at least a token figure from the business community.

The most conspicuous omission of all was, of course, the Japanese emperor. After World War I the Allies had sought to punish Kaiser Wilhelm II. The Japanese emperor may not have played so important a role in World War II as had Wilhelm in World War I, but he was *de jure* sovereign, and he had participated in many of the crucial decisions of the war. Why was he not indicted? Horwitz reported the emperor's exclusion from the indictment as follows: "A study of the Emperor's role in Japan's

[73] Horwitz, "Tokyo Trial," p. 498.

aggression was made from two different points of view—his role in the governmental machinery of Japan, and his personal role in supporting or objecting to the aggressive policy of his advisers. A study of the governmental machinery from both the point of view of theory and of operation showed the Emperor's role to be that of a figurehead."[74] The Executive Committee actually may have conducted such a study and arrived at this conclusion, but the decision not to prosecute the emperor was made by other people on other grounds long before the Executive Committee began its work.

In his *Reminiscences* General MacArthur claimed principal credit for the decision. The initial list of war criminals was headed by the emperor, and Great Britain and the Soviet Union (and Australia, China, and New Zealand)[75] urged his prosecution. Wrote MacArthur: "Realizing the tragic consequences that would follow from such an unjust action, I had stoutly resisted such efforts. When Washington seemed to be veering toward the British point of view, I had advised that I would need at least one mil-

[74] *Ibid.*, p. 497. The account of Chief Prosecutor Keenan's private secretary, Yamazaki Seiichi, indicates that the Executive Committee was asked only for its consent. Keenan reported to the committee that the emperor would not be indicted. The British Associate Prosecutor asked immediately: "Is that a decision? Or is it a proposal?" Keenan replied: "The policy has been decided. I am asking your agreement." The Briton retorted: "I can't go along with that kind of thing." Keenan fired back: "It is in the interest of all the Allied nations to carry out occupation policy smoothly; that is also the will of SCAP. Therefore if you gentlemen are unable to agree with SCAP policy, feel free to pack your bags and go home." Retranslated from the Japanese, Yamazaki Seiichi, "Keenan kosaku no himitsu," *Nihon shuho*, 493:9.
[75] *Facts on File*, v (1945), 358G; vi (1946), 21G.

lion reinforcements should such action be taken. I believed that if the emperor was indicted, and perhaps hanged, as a war criminal, military government would have to be instituted throughout all Japan, and guerrilla warfare would probably break out. The emperor's name had then been stricken from the list."[76] MacArthur gave no date for this decision, but he spoke in the past tense as if the decision had been made before his first meeting with the emperor late in September 1945. As MacArthur indicated, the final decision was made in Washington, but there is some doubt as to the date. One source mentions an order of October 6, 1945 from the Joint Chiefs of Staff to start the trials quickly but not to involve the emperor.[77] In 1949 the U.S. State Department revealed that a secret order had gone out from the U.S. Joint Chiefs of Staff in January 1946 not to indict the emperor.[78] By Horwitz' own account, the Executive Committee of the prosecution at Tokyo began its selection of defendants in mid-February 1946.[79] In April the Far Eastern Commission supported the decision not to try the emperor.[80]

[76] Douglas MacArthur, *Reminiscences* (New York: McGraw-Hill, 1964), pp. 287-288.

[77] Harry Emerson Wildes, *Typhoon in Tokyo* (New York: Macmillan, 1954), p. 77.

[78] *Facts on File*, IX (1949), 20A: "The U.S. State Department added Jan. 14 that all 11 of Japan's enemies, including Russia, agreed to exempt Hirohito to facilitate Japan's surrender and occupation of the country."

[79] Horwitz, "Tokyo Trial," p. 495.

[80] Department of State *Bulletin*, 22.554:244 (Feb. 13, 1950); *Activities of the Far Eastern Commission*, Feb. 26, 1946 to July 10, 1947, Report by the Secretary General (Washington: U.S. Government Printing Office, 1947), Appendix 39, p. 98.

The decision to exclude the emperor was a political decision, not a decision based upon the merits of the case. Under the concept of conspiracy invoked by the prosecution, it would have been easy to assure the conviction of the emperor on all the counts of the indictment. Consider the remarkable statements Chief Prosecutor Keenan made in 1950 on the Mutual Broadcasting Company's "Meet the Press" program. Should the emperor have been tried? "My answer to that, briefly is no. From the evidence at the trial, it was quite clear that Hirohito himself did not want war." Could he have been tried? "Strictly legally, Emperor Hirohito could have been tried and convicted, because under the Constitution of Japan, he did have the power to make war and stop it. We could have convicted him."[81] The evidence indicated that the emperor "did not want war," yet he could have been convicted as a war criminal.

Consider also the emperor's statement to General MacArthur at their first meeting. As MacArthur reported it, the emperor said: "I come to you, General MacArthur, to offer myself to the judgment of the powers you represent as the one to bear sole responsibility for every political and military decision made and action taken by my people in the conduct of the war."[82] This is not to say that the emperor was guilty of war crimes. It is to say that if the Tokyo defendants were guilty, then so also was their emperor.

There is even one report that the prosecution went to great lengths to insure that the emperor was not implicated at all in testimony before the tribunal. At one point in his testimony, this account goes, Tojo commented that

[81] "Joseph B. Keenan Meets the Press," *American Mercury*, LXX, 316:456-459 (April 1950).
[82] MacArthur, *Reminiscences*, p. 288.

no Japanese ever opposed the imperial will. In consterna-
tion at the ramifications of that statement, Chief Prosecutor Keenan requested the Imperial Household to exert its
influence on Tojo to change his testimony.[83] If that report

[83] This incident deserves an extended note. The basic account is
that of Yamazaki Seiichi, private secretary to Chief Prosecutor
Keenan during the trial. Keenan was upset, so Yamazaki writes,
by the following exchange:

Tojo: "And I further wish to add that there is no Japanese subject who would go against the will of His Majesty; more particularly, among high officials of the Japanese government or of
Japan." . . .

Webb: "Well, you know the implications from that reply." (*Proceedings*, p. 36,521.)

Keenan, prosecution witness Tanaka (see Appendix 5), and
Yamazaki met late that same evening to discuss means of repair-
ing the damage. They contrived an elaborate plan, complete with
an Imperial Household intermediary and coded phone calls, to
convince Tojo of the need to leave a less ambiguous impression of
the emperor's stance. The plan succeeded, writes Yamazaki, and
resulted in the following exchange in open court one week later:

Keenan: "While we are discussing the subject matter of Emper-
ors [the questioning had concerned Emperor Pu Yi of Manchukuo,
and what follows is clearly a digression], it might be an appropriate moment to ask you a few questions on the relative positions
of yourself and the Emperor of Japan on the matter of waging war
in December of 1941. You have told us that the Emperor on repeated occasions made known to you that he was a man of peace
and did not want war, is that correct?"

Tojo: "I was then speaking to you of my feeling towards the
Emperor as a subject, and that is quite a different matter from
the problem of responsibility, that is, the responsibility of the
Emperor."

Keenan: "Well, you did make war against the United States,
Great Britain, and the Netherlands, did you not?"

Tojo: "War was decided on in my cabinet."

Keenan: "Was that the will of Emperor Hirohito, that war
should be instituted?"

Tojo: "It may not have been according to his will, but it is a

114

is true, it speaks eloquently of the strong political concern (and weak professional ethics) of the prosecution.

From the point of view of common sense, the emperor was implicated throughout the trial. He had attended many of the crucial conferences. Almost all the accused had been his officials, his advisors. In September 1945 he rejected a list of war criminals drawn up by the Japanese Government in anticipation of Allied arrests, saying that the men listed had "served earnestly and with great loyalty."[84] Although that list and the Tokyo trial list were

---

fact that because of my advice and because of the advice given by the High Command the Emperor consented, though reluctantly, to the war."

Interpreter: "The first part should be corrected: It might have been against the Emperor's will."

Tojo (continuing): "The Emperor's love for and desire for peace remained the same right up to the very moment when hostilities commenced, and even during the war his feelings remained the same. The Emperor's feelings in this regard can be clearly ascertained from the Imperial Rescript given on the 8th of December, 1941 declaring war. That portion of the Rescript was included because of the Emperor's wishes on the responsibility of the government. That is to say, the Imperial Rescript contains words to this effect: This war is indeed unavoidable and is against my own desires." (*Proceedings*, 36,779-36,781.)

For Yamazaki's account, see his "Keenan kosaku," pp. 11-16.

At the trial's close Tojo's Japanese lawyer reported "Tojo's mind is eased very much by the verdict, knowing that he has given no additional trouble to the Emperor" (*New York Times*, Nov. 13, 1948, p. 9).

[84] Kido diary, quoted in Kojima, *Tokyo saiban*, I, 35. Kido quotes the emperor's expression of opposition to the proposal that Japan herself conduct war crimes trials: "Those whom the enemy regards as war criminals, in particular those whom the enemy holds responsible [for the war], are all men who served earnestly and with great loyalty. Hence, it would be unbearable to judge them in the name of the emperor."

115

certainly not identical, the emperor probably would have made the same statement concerning the Tokyo defendants. Almost all had been his advisors. It would take the utmost sophistry to justify, on the one hand, the conviction of the emperor's closest advisors and, on the other, the failure even to indict the emperor. As it was, the emperor was not even called to testify at the trial.[85]

This anomaly was not lost on two of the justices. In arguing for commutation of the death sentences, President Webb cited the fact that the emperor had not been indicted. Wrote Webb: "The authority of the emperor was proved beyond question when he ended the war. The outstanding part played by him in starting as well as ending it was the subject of evidence led by the prosecution.. . . . It is, of course, for the prosecution to say who will be indicted; but a British Court in passing sentence would, I believe, take into account, if it could, that the leader in the crime, though available for trial, had been granted immunity. . . ." Justice Webb continued: "I do not suggest the emperor should have been prosecuted. That is beyond my province. His immunity was, no doubt, decided upon in the best interests of all the Allied Powers." Because the

[85] Japanese commentators have even suggested that President Webb's recall to Australia in November 1947 was contrived by Keenan and MacArthur in order to have the issue of the emperor's testifying decided in his absence. Webb was convinced of the emperor's guilt and hostile to Keenan; he presumably wished to have the emperor testify. His interim replacement, appointed by General MacArthur at that time, was General Cramer of the United States. Presumably he was more malleable. Takikawa Masajiro, *Tokyo saiban o sabaku* (Tokyo: Towasha, 1952), pp. 250-254; Uematsu Keita, *Kyokuto kokusai gunji saiban* (Tokyo: Jimbutsu oraisha, 1962), pp. 86-89.

116

emperor had not been indicted, however, none of his ministers should suffer the death penalty.[86]

Justice Bernard of France held that the failure to indict the emperor was a serious defect, one of three that nullified the trial. He argued that the evidence brought forward at the trial had implicated the emperor; the emperor "could have been counted among the suspects." Indeed, the emperor was not merely a suspect. Of the Japanese declaration of war in December 1941 Bernard wrote: "It cannot be denied, it [the declaration] had a principal author who escaped all prosecution and of whom in any case the present Defendants could only be considered as accomplices." Bernard then agreed with Webb that the emperor's absence from the trial "was certainly detrimental to the defense of the accused."[87] Surprisingly, the Russian justice held his peace.[88] Kid gloves for the emperor, but the treatment of "common felons" (Keenan's term in his Opening Statement)[89] for the emperor's ministers.

During the trial President Webb had quizzed Chief Prosecutor Keenan on this failure to indict the emperor. Keenan replied that the prosecution was proceeding on the theory that the "emperor had been in the power of 'gangsters.'"[90] Given the confines within which it had to operate, the prosecution could hardly think otherwise.

[86] Webb, "Separate Opinion," pp. 18-19.

[87] Bernard, "Dissenting Judgment," pp. 19, 22, 19.

[88] In 1950 the U.S.S.R. formally proposed the reopening of the International Military Tribunal for the Far East to try other war criminals including specifically the emperor (Department of State *Bulletin*, 22.554:224 [Feb. 13, 1950]). Communist China seconded this suggestion (*New York Times*, Dec. 16, 1950, p. 2).

[89] "Trial of Japanese War Criminals," p. 3.

[90] *New York Times*, Jan. 14, 1949, p. 11. I have been unable to locate this exchange in the trial record.

117

4. Rules of Evidence

Article 13 of the Tokyo Charter (virtually identical with its Nuremberg counterpart) read in part as follows: "The tribunal shall not be bound by technical rules of evidence. It shall adopt and apply to the greatest possible extent expeditious and non-technical procedure, and shall admit any evidence which it deems to have probative value." A clause similar to this appears in the first American draft of the Nuremberg Charter.[91] Robert H. Jackson introduced this clause at London with the following words: "We do not want technical rules of evidence designed for jury trials to be used in this case to cut down what is really and fairly of probative value, and so we propose to lay down as a part of the statute that utmost liberality shall be used."[92] Three days later the British spokesman voiced his support: "That makes clear that it is for the tribunal to decide whether the evidence has value in the direction of proof even though a national code might not allow proof in that form."[93]

Common law systems differ from civil law systems in their provisions for evidence. Article 13 is not completely out of line with Continental practice, in which much broader rules of evidence are standard. What is surprising is the ease with which the representatives of Great Britain and the United States acceded in—indeed, proposed—the abandonment of their domestic rules. The reaction of Justice Pal, trained in British law, is eloquent: "In prescribing the rules of evidence for this trial *the Charter practi-*

[91] "American Draft of Definitive Proposal, presented to Foreign Ministers at San Francisco, April 1945," *London Conference*, p. 25.
[92] *London Conference*, p. 83.   [93] *Ibid.*, p. 100.

118

cally discarded all the procedural rules devised by the various national systems of law, based on litigious experience and tradition, to guard a tribunal against erroneous persuasion, and thus left us, in the matter of proof, to guide ourselves independently of any artificial rules of procedure."[94]

Why did the representatives of common law systems favor this article? Jackson might have cited domestic procedure in conspiracy trials, where as we have seen rules of procedure are looser than in normal trials. This he did not do. His only justification at London was that rules of evidence designed to protect juries untrained in the law would be superfluous for judges well trained in the law; indeed, "technical rules of evidence" might hamper proof. At the Tokyo trial President Webb stated the same thought repeatedly: ". . . we are not a jury, but judges; and . . . we can be trusted to hear things that might prejudice a jury but which would not influence us."[95] On the basis of their performance we may doubt whether the justices at Tokyo were worthy of such trust.

Article 13 went on to specify admissible evidence "without limiting in any way the scope of the foregoing general rules." This evidence included affidavits, diaries, and documents "including sworn or unsworn statements." Affidavits offer two problems for jurists trained in the common law. First, the court has no control over the process in which lawyer and witness formulate an affidavit. Sec-

[94] Pal, *Judgment*, p. 139. Italics are Justice Pal's.

[95] *Proceedings*, p. 7,204. Again (p. 7,836): "I do ask you to remember, we are not a jury; we are eleven judges trained in the law, trained to give decisions, trained to weigh evidence."

119

ond, unless the witness takes the stand, the content of the affidavit is not subject to cross-examination.[96] Diaries and unsworn documents pose even more serious problems.

Consider some of the evidence admitted at the Tokyo trial. There were press releases offered by the prosecution, although the tribunal rejected press releases offered by the defense. There was a conversation with a person since deceased. There were letters from private Japanese citizens to the War Ministry; these the defense denounced as "crank letters."[97]

We might conclude that very little evidence was rejected. But this was not the case. Justice Pal made a list:

"1. Evidence relating to the state of affairs in China prior to the time when the Japanese armed forces began to operate;

"2. The evidence showing that the Japanese forces in China restored peace and tranquillity there; It was observed in this connection that 'none of the accused will be exculpated merely because it is shown, if it is shown, that the Japanese forces in China restored peace and tranquillity there. What you must establish . . . is that the Japanese armed forces . . . had authority or justification or excuse for what they did.'. . .

"5. (a) Evidence as to the relations between the U.S.S.R. and Finland, Latvia, Esthonia, Poland, and Roumania.

(b) Evidence as to the relations between the U.S. and Denmark vis-à-vis Greenland and Iceland. . . .

"6. Evidence relating to A-Bomb decision.

"7. Evidence regarding the Reservation by the Several States while signing the Pact of Paris. . . ."

The prosecution's case, thought Pal, rested on inference

[96] Pal, *Judgment*, pp. 148-149.
[97] Appleman, *Military Tribunals*, pp. 252-254.

from circumstantial evidence to establish the conspiracy. Hence, the defense might disprove this inference by explaining the events in question.[98] But the tribunal chose not to admit important elements of any such explanation: witness items 1 and 2.

Perhaps the most unsettling aspect of the tribunal's procedure was its very uncertainness. No one could be sure what the rules were. Consider the account of one student of procedure at international military tribunals:

"One of the more interesting occurrences arose with reference to John B. Powell's book, *My 25 Years in China*. Powell had been called as a witness for the prosecution. The defense then sought to introduce excerpts from his book. The tribunal originally inferred that this would be admissible, but then changed the rule and excluded such evidence. Defense counsel Logan remonstrated with the tribunal and was roughly reprimanded by the president. Almost immediately thereafter a different book was offered with a similar attitude shown by the president. One of the members of the tribunal then requested a conference and court recessed. Upon reconvening, this offer was also rejected. Mr. Logan then reoffered other excerpts from such books and a discussion ensued. They were rejected on the president casting his own ballot to break a tie. Then Logan offered Powell's book, and it was admitted. Other documents were rejected subsequently, but, after the president had announced rejection of one document on his casting a vote, he received another vote from a member of the tribunal and was forced to change his ruling."[99]

[98] Pal, *Judgment*, pp. 156-160.
[99] Appleman, *Military Tribunals*, pp. 253-254.

Halfway through the trial the tribunal introduced a rule of best evidence (that the best, the most authentic, evidence must be produced). As Justice Pal commented: "... in a proceeding where we had to allow the prosecution to bring in any amount of hearsay evidence, it was somewhat *misplaced caution* to introduce this best evidence rule, particularly when it operated practically against the defense only."[100] Such were the consequences of the rules of evidence in force at Tokyo and of the "large and somewhat unpredictable discretion" (Jackson's phrase)[101] these rules bestowed on the court.

At Tokyo the justices were selected only from the aggrieved and victor nations. No challenge to their credentials, collective or individual, was allowed. They were themselves the judges of their own qualifications and their own attendance. A bare majority constituted a quorum; and a majority of that quorum could make all decisions to come before the tribunal.

The indictment covered only Japanese acts and individuals, but similar acts had been committed by many of the prosecuting nations. A "representative" group of Japanese leaders stood accused, but the process that selected them was not without its arbitrary aspects.

The rules of evidence at the tribunal deprived the defendants of procedural safeguards cherished in common law practice. Further, these rules were applied more

[100] Pal, *Judgment*, p. 154. Italics are Justice Pal's. See also T'sai, "Judicial Administration," vi, 33 and notes.

[101] *London Conference*, xi. For one legal observer's list of ten procedural flaws at Tokyo, see Gordon Ireland, "Uncommon Law in Martial Tokyo," *Yearbook of World Affairs* (London: Stevens and Sons), 4:86-87 (1950).

strictly against the defense than against the prosecution. All these procedural matters played their part in the judgment of the Tokyo tribunal: death to 7 defendants, life imprisonment to 16, and twenty years and seven years to the remaining 2.

The rules of evidence at the Tokyo trial functioned to facilitate the prosecution and impede the defense. But we should guard against the automatic assumption that better rules of evidence, a fairer trial, would have changed the verdict. As Arthur M. Schlesinger wrote of the Sacco-Vanzetti case: "Myths to the contrary notwithstanding, judicial processes do not take place in a social void; judges are men, not gods. The strict observance of legal forms does not necessarily assure the accused of a fair trial."[102]

Consider also the argument of Jessica Mitford about the Spock trial: "Is it not self-deluding to speak in terms of a 'fair trial' in a politically motivated, politically timed, and politically organized prosecution? When applied to such a case, does not the cherished concept of due process of law, the foundation of our system of jurisprudence, become merely an elaborate sham to mask what is in reality a convenient device to silence opponents to governmental policies? If this is so, does not the demand for fair trial and due process in political cases simply help perpetuate the myth—should not the demand rather be, in the public interest, an *end* to political trials?"[103]

At the Tokyo trial a majority verdict similar to Justice Pal's—all accused innocent of all charges—was from the

[102] Arthur M. Schlesinger, "Introduction," in G. Louis Jouchin and Edmund M. Morgan, *The Legacy of Sacco and Vanzetti* (New York: Harcourt, Brace and Co., 1948), p. xvi; somewhat altered in Mitford, *Dr. Spock*, p. 239.

[103] Mitford, *Dr. Spock*, p. 238.

beginning virtually unthinkable. To hold that the rules of evidence alone were at fault would surely be deluding ourselves, protecting us from a recognition of the greater inequities of the Tokyo trial. In this sense the statement during the trial of President Webb, that "We are giving them a much better trial than we would have had were the conditions reversed,"[104] is wholly irrelevant.

[104] Cunningham, "Address," p. 34. This statement I was unable to locate in the *Proceedings*.

124

V.

PROBLEMS OF HISTORY

> . . . at the Tokyo trial it was
> remarkable to note the similar-
> ity of the patterns of the dicta-
> tors whether those of the Nazis,
> Fascists, or exponents of imperial
> rule in Japan. Whether it was
> Hitler, Mussolini, or Tojo their
> techniques were alike as peas in
> a pod.
> —Joseph B. Keenan, 1949

> The story here has been pushed
> a little too far, perhaps, to give it
> a place in the Hitler series.
> —Justice Radhabinod Pal,
> November, 1948

WE HAVE discussed the shaky basis of the Tokyo trial in international law. We have examined several fundamental procedural flaws. Invalid law or faulty procedure: either of these alone can provide legal grounds for throwing out a court's decision. As Justice Bernard wrote in his dissent: "A verdict reached by a tribunal after a defective procedure cannot be a valid one."[1]

But for non-legal minds—and that includes the author and probably most of his audience—there is a third important approach to the Tokyo trial: the historical approach. For us the validity of the Tokyo trial depends in large part

[1] Bernard, "Dissenting Judgment," p. 20.

125

on the historical worth of its verdict. Does that verdict, we ask, meet minimal tests of historical accuracy? Even the most biased panel of justices, invoking the most questionable interpretation of international law and following the most dubious procedures, might have arrived at a reasonably accurate picture of prewar events in Japan and in the Pacific. But if the verdict cannot stand historical scrutiny, then for us the trial loses its last claim to our respect.

Historical accuracy was an important motive behind the trials at Nuremberg and Tokyo. The American Government had called for trials rather than for executive action in part to "make available for all mankind to study in future years an authentic record of Nazi crimes and criminality."[2] Speaking shortly after the Tokyo trial ended, Chief Prosecutor Keenan also stressed this point: "I think that the foremost service they [the Tokyo trial] rendered was to establish the facts authentically, particularly with the Japanese people."[3]

The writing of official history was an important motive at Nuremberg and at Tokyo. But such a motive is not a proper legal motive. Consider the words of Hannah Arendt: "The purpose of a trial is to render justice, and nothing else; even the noblest of ulterior purposes—'the making of a record of the Hitler regime which would withstand the test of history,' as Robert G. Storey, executive trial counsel at Nuremberg, formulated the supposed higher aims of the Nuremberg Trials—can only detract

---

[2] *London Conference*, p. 6.

[3] "Joseph B. Keenan Meets the Press," p. 458. See also Defense Counsel Cunningham's statement: "The purpose of the trial was to convince the Japanese people that their leaders misled them into war . . ." ("Address," p. 34).

126

from the law's main business: to weigh the charges brought against the accused, to render judgment, and to mete out due punishment."[4] Judge Charles E. Wyzanski, Jr., has stated the same thought in fewer words: ". . . to regard a trial as a propaganda device is to debase justice."[5]

Nevertheless, the majority judgment at Tokyo did seek to write the definitive history of the prewar years. It devoted 1,050 pages of its judgment—out of 1,218 pages in all—to findings of fact. It was on the basis of these facts that the majority judgment found the Japanese leaders guilty of conspiracy to commit aggression and guilty also of aggression itself. But how does this judgment look twenty-three years later? Is it compelling in its historical logic? Or is it open to severe challenge?

1. Overall Conspiracy

Count 1 of the indictment read: "All the accused together with other persons, between the 1st January, 1928, and the 2nd September, 1945, participated as leaders, organizers, instigators, or accomplices in the formulation or execution of a common plan or conspiracy, and are responsible for all acts performed by any person in execution of such plan." This conspiracy had as its object the domination of East Asia, the Pacific and Indian Oceans, and all countries bordering on them.[6] We have seen already that the judgment restricted this object to "East Asia, the Western and South Western Pacific Ocean and the Indian Ocean, and certain of the islands in these oceans."[7] But the tribunal did find that a conspiracy with this narrower

[4] Hannah Arendt, *Eichmann in Jerusalem*, rev. ed. (New York: Viking, 1964), p. 252.
[5] Wyzanski, *Whereas*, p. 175.
[6] "Trial of Japanese War Criminals," p. 47.
[7] *Judgment*, p. 1,137. See also Appendix 2.

object had existed, and that 23 of the 25 accused were parties to it.

The judgment read in part: "Already prior to 1928 Okawa, one of the original defendants . . . was publicly advocating that Japan should extend her territory on the Continent of Asia by the threat or, if necessary, by use of military force. . . . Already when Tanaka was premier, from 1927 to 1929, a party of military men, with Okawa and other civilian supporters, was advocating this policy of Okawa's that Japan should expand by the use of force. The conspiracy was now in being. It remained in being until Japan's defeat in 1945."[8]

The judgment then discussed Japan's plans for war, from 1931 in Manchuria to 1937 in China to the war that never took place against the Soviet Union (see below) to the attacks of December 7 and 8, 1941. Said the judgment: "These far-reaching plans for waging wars of aggression, and the prolonged and intricate preparation for and waging of these wars of aggression, were not the work of one man. They were the work of many leaders acting in pursuance of a common plan for the achievement of a common object. That common object, that they should secure Japan's domination by preparing and waging wars of aggression, was a criminal object."[9]

Part of the problem in dealing with the charge of conspiracy is that conspiracy means one thing to lawyers (Anglo-American lawyers, that is) and quite another to everyone else. As we noted in Chapter III conspiracy in the legal sense does not demand that there be a concrete plan of action. Nor is any actual wrongdoing necessary: the crime lies in the intent. Nor must the conspirators be

[8] *Judgment*, p. 1,138.   [9] *Ibid.*, p. 1,142.

128

known to each other. Nor must there be secrecy. Little wonder, then, at the complaint of an English lawyer: "No intelligible definition of 'conspiracy' has yet been established."[10] To most non-lawyers, however, conspiracy means what a dictionary says it means: "an evil, unlawful, treacherous, or surreptitious plan formulated in secret by two or more persons."[11] Secrecy, the existence of a plan, and actual collaboration among the conspirators are all crucial elements here. Clearly not all legal conspiracies qualify as historical or common-sense conspiracies. In the following discussion it is the historical, garden-variety conspiracy with which we concern ourselves.

The definitive history of prewar Japan has not yet been written. Nevertheless, it seems already clear that there was no historical conspiracy even remotely similar to the conspiracy described in the majority judgment.[12] There was in Japan no Nazi Party, no disciplined clique seeking first to subvert the government at home and then to embark on foreign adventures. The Japanese Government in the period of the indictment was without a unifying planning group, without even a Hitler. Tojo came the closest. For a while during the war he was Prime Minister, War Minister, and Army Chief of Staff. But consider these facts.

[10] Quoted in Mitford, *Trial of Dr. Spock*, p. 62.

[11] *Random House Dictionary of the English Language* (New York: Random House, 1967), p. 313.

[12] For recent American scholarship on this period see: Butow, *Japan's Decision* and *Tojo*; James B. Crowley, *Japan's Quest for Autonomy* (Princeton: Princeton University Press, 1966); Nobutaka Ike, *Japan's Decision for War: Records of the 1941 Policy Conferences* (Stanford: Stanford University Press, 1967); Akira Iriye, *After Imperialism* (Cambridge: Harvard University Press, 1965); and Sadako N. Ogata, *Defiance in Manchuria* (Berkeley: University of California Press, 1964).

Tojo lacked a political party of his own; he came to power and comported himself in power quite legally; and he fell from power more than a year before the war ended. Wrote Justice Pal: "The case of the present accused before us cannot in any way be likened to the case either of Napoleon or of Hitler. The constitution of Japan was fully working. The Sovereign, the Army, and the civil officials all remained connected as usual and in normal ways with the society. The constitution of the state remained fashioned as before in relation to the will of the society. The public opinion was in full vigor. The society was not in the least deprived of any of its means to make its will effective. These accused came to power constitutionally and only to work the machinery provided by the constitution. They remained all along amenable to public opinion, and even during war, the public opinion truly and vigorously functioned. . . . These persons did not usurp any power. . . ."[13] We may quibble with Justice Pal on a few of his points, but not on the main outlines of his argument.

To be sure, there had been conspiracies and plots galore in the early 1930's, and several defendants had been involved. There had also been unauthorized action in Manchuria by elements of the army. Finally, there had been the rebellion in Tokyo of February 26, 1936. These events did bear some superficial resemblance to the early history of the Nazis. But contemporary historians agree that there was a break between the early 1930's and the later years. The February rebellion precipitated a purge of army extremists, and after 1936 army discipline held. Ironically, Tojo himself was instrumental in restoring this discipline.[14] Thereafter, the army did formulate ambitious

[13] Pal, *Judgment*, p. 698.   [14] Butow, *Tojo*, pp. 73-74.

plans for the expansion of Japanese power; and the army did use the spectre of further insurrection as an argument in favor of adopting its proposals. But even after 1936 there was no meeting of minds among the defendants, no concrete plan for Japan to follow, no single decision (until late 1941) which led inevitably to Pearl Harbor and war.

Nevertheless, the prosecution argued the existence of a conspiracy, and the majority judgment found that there had been one. Was not the whole idea incredible? No, urged the prosecution, it might seem incredible but it was not: "One of the difficulties in relation to the analysis of this conspiracy is that it was of such breadth of scope that it is difficult to conceive of its being undertaken by a group of human beings." The prosecution went on to assert: ". . . none of the events which took place during this fourteen-year period occurred by accident. Every event was coldly calculated, planned for, and put into execution."[15] That is arrant nonsense, of course. Yet the majority judgment did lump together Okawa's ultranationalist essays of the mid-1920's, the Mukden Incident of 1931, the assassination of Prime Minister Inukai in 1932, the rebellion of 1936, the war in China, the Axis Alliance, and the decisions of 1941. It laid the responsibility for all these events at the door of the conspiracy and of those conspirators on trial before it.

It is even questionable whether we can use the term "conspiracy" regarding the Tojo cabinet itself. Its first foreign minister joined the cabinet on Tojo's assurance that one last effort would be made to reach diplomatic settlement with the United States.[16] Its third foreign minister, Shigemitsu, joined the cabinet in wartime with the spe-

[15] *Proceedings*, pp. 38,972-38,973.   [16] *Judgment*, pp. 1,204-1,205.

cific aim of negotiating peace.[17] For the Tokyo majority, the former was a conspirator but the latter was not.[18]

There is also cogent objection to the method in which the Tokyo majority established the existence of the conspiracy. To quote Justice Pal: ". . . no direct evidence of the fact to be proved could be presented to us. . . ."[19] Instead, the method of proof necessarily was one of inference, of inferring the existence of a conspiracy from a set of events. In Justice Pal's words: "As I have already pointed out, there is no direct evidence of this conspiracy or design. The factum of this alleged conspiracy, design, or plan has not been attested to directly by any witness, thing, or document. By evidence the prosecution has sought to establish certain *intermediate facts* which, according to it, are sufficiently proximate to the principal fact to be proved, so as to be receivable as evidentiary of it."[20]

However, Justice Pal contended that each fact upon which the prosecution and the judgment relied as evidence of the existence of a conspiracy could be explained without postulating the existence of a conspiracy. To be sure, the tribunal itself had excluded some of the evidence relevant to such an explanation: for example, conditions in China prior to the Manchurian incident, or Japanese fears of international communism. But even the evidence before the tribunal admitted of several explanations, not simply the inference of conspiracy favored by the judgment. In four hundred pages of his opinion Justice Pal set forth his explanation of the facts before the tribunal. He

[17] Röling, "Opinion," p. 228.
[18] The majority judgment found Shigemitsu not guilty of conspiracy but guilty of waging aggressive war during his tenure as foreign minister in the Tojo cabinet. *Judgment*, pp. 1,193-1,194. See also Appendix 5.
[19] Pal, *Judgment*, p. 180.   [20] *Ibid.*, p. 558. Italics in original.

found that the existence of a conspiracy had not been proved.[21] In concluding his argument against the existence of a conspiracy, Justice Pal wrote what may well be the best epitaph for the Tokyo trial as a whole: "The story here has been pushed a little too far, perhaps, to give it a place in the Hitler series."[22]

Consider also the opinion of Justice Bernard. He wrote: "No direct proof was furnished concerning the formation among individuals known, on a known date, at a specific point, of a plot the object of which was to assure to Japan the domination . . . of some part of the world." What had been proved was only ". . . the existence among certain influential classes of the Japanese nation of the desire to seat at all costs the domination of Japan upon other parts of East Asia." But this alone was not enough. Continued Bernard: ". . . the question remains completely to ascertain whether by doing this they did or did not act criminally. The question was neither raised by the prosecution nor answered by the judgment of the majority."[23]

The majority judgment set out to write the history of a seventeen-year period of modern history. Involved in that period were great historical trends: Japan's emergence to world-power status, the continued instability of China, the growth of American power and ambition in the Pacific, the economic crisis of the 1930's, the rigidity of prevailing ideas of international order. But these trends the majority judgment ignored or distorted in favor of a simplistic concept of conspiracy.[24] How comforting an idea, but how fallacious!

[21] *Ibid.*, p. 562.   [22] *Ibid.*, p. 382.
[23] Bernard, "Dissenting Judgment," pp. 21-22.
[24] Paul W. Schroeder, *The Axis Alliance and Japanese-American Relations, 1941* (Ithaca: Cornell University Press, 1958), pp. 218-219.

The question of conspiracy leads us directly to one fundamental flaw, perhaps *the* fundamental flaw, of the whole Tokyo trial. The idea of an international military tribunal, the concepts of international law that tribunal was asked to invoke, the view that World War II had been a dark plot against civilization—all these had emerged from the Allied reaction to the acts of Nazi Germany. Those acts were indeed hideous. They demanded retribution of some kind. But Japan was not Germany; Tojo was not Hitler; the Pacific war was not identical with the European war. Yet in spite of these crucial differences the legal trappings set up to punish the Nazis were applied in precisely the same manner to the Japanese leaders. Whether the miscarriage of justice at Tokyo affects decisively our evaluation of Nuremberg is a matter for philosophers and lawyers. There can be no doubt, however, that the categories and assumptions of Nuremberg broke down completely in their application at Tokyo—broke down, that is, so long as the tribunal was not prepared to consider a verdict of not guilty.

2. *Relations between Japan and the Soviet Union*

The Soviet Union attacked Japan in August 1945. We have already suggested already that this attack constituted aggression under the Pact of Paris, as well as a war "in violation of international . . . treaties" described in the Tokyo Charter. But the tribunal did not consider the Soviet attack either as a separate topic or as relevant evidence to help determine what constituted aggression and what constituted acceptable use of coercion in the international community of World War II.

Far from condemning the Soviet Union for its attack on Japan, the Tokyo majority found Japan guilty of aggression against the Soviet Union. Ten counts of the indictment had concerned Japanese action against the U.S.S.R.; and three counts had dealt with Japanese action against the Mongolian People's Republic. These counts, taken together, included three of conspiracy, seven of aggression, and three of conventional war crimes.

The majority judgment reduced these thirteen counts to five. But on all five of these, Japan was held guilty: on the basic count of conspiracy, on two specific cases of aggression (the Lake Khassan and Nomonhan incidents), and on two counts of conventional war crimes.

The evidence cited by the judgment in support of its finding on Count 1 covered fifty pages. It was curious evidence. It included a statement by the civilian and private citizen Okawa from 1924, various references by Japanese officials to the inevitability of conflict with the Soviet Union, and the national policy statement (August 1936) of the Hirota cabinet. It drew an inference from the Japanese rejection in the early 1930's of the Soviet offer of a non-aggression pact: ". . . Japan rejected the proposal in spite of the fact that the Japanese Government had assurances at that time that it was a sincere expression of peaceful policy of the Soviet Union in the Far East."[25] Since the Soviet Union's offer was "sincere," and the Japanese response was negative, the inference the majority judgment drew was that the Japanese had aggressive intentions against the Soviet Union.

The judgment considered the Neutrality Pact of April 13, 1941 between the Soviet Union and Japan, but mainly

[25] *Judgment*, p. 780.

135

to cast aspersions on Japan's intentions on entering into the pact and her subsequent behavior under the pact. Japan had declined such a pact in the 1930's, but her acceptance in 1941 was no change in basic policy: "This willingness . . . did not indicate any change of the Japanese attitude towards the U.S.S.R., nor any abatement of her acquisitive designs upon that country."[26]

Indeed, the Neutrality Pact furthered Japan's aggressive designs: "It would appear that Japan was not sincere in concluding the Neutrality Pact with the U.S.S.R., but considering her agreements with Germany more advantageous, she signed the Neutrality Pact to facilitate her plans for an attack upon the U.S.S.R. . . . Japan's 'neutrality' in the war between Germany and the U.S.S.R. in reality served and seems to have been designed to serve as a screen for such aid as she could give Germany pending her own attack upon the U.S.S.R."[27]

But of course the tribunal could not find that Japan had broken the pact, because between 1941 and 1945 there were no hostilities of any kind between Japan and the Soviet Union. Japan's aid to Germany included maintaining a large force in Manchuria (and thus tying up Russian troops), forwarding military intelligence, shelling several Soviet ships (number unspecified) in a single month, and arresting and detaining "on occasion for lengthy periods" other Soviet ships, presumably in the same month (unspecified) in 1941.[28]

On the basis of this evidence the tribunal found Japan guilty of conspiracy to wage aggressive war against the U.S.S.R. The verdict read: ". . . they [the conspirators]

[26] *Ibid.*, p. 819.   [27] *Ibid.*, p. 823.   [28] *Ibid.*, pp. 823-826.

had long been planning and preparing a war of aggression which they proposed to launch against the U.S.S.R. The intention was to seize that country's Eastern territories when a favourable opportunity occurred."[29] But then the verdict admitted that that favorable opportunity never occurred. It said: "Their proposed attack on the U.S.S.R. was postponed from time to time for various reasons, among which were (1) Japan's preoccupation with the war in China, which was absorbing unexpectedly large military resources, and (2) Germany's pact of non-aggression with the U.S.S.R. in 1939, which for the time freed the U.S.S.R. from threat of attack on her Western frontier, and might have allowed her to devote the bulk of her strength to the defence of her Eastern territories if Japan had attacked here."[30]

To be sure, the Japanese had not attacked the Soviet Union, but that fact was immaterial to the charge of conspiracy. As we have seen, the majority judgment found Japan guilty of conspiracy to wage aggression against the Soviet Union.

In the entire period from 1928 to August 1945 only two military engagements between Japan and the Soviet Union took place. These were the Lake Khassan incident of 1938 and the Nomonhan incident of 1939. At stake in both incidents were Japanese demands for "rectification" of boundaries, rectifications that would have improved greatly Japan's military position along the frontiers involved. The Lake Khassan incident lasted twelve days, from July 31 to August 11, 1938; it ended in Japanese defeat. The tribunal found Japan to blame for the incident and concluded: "Though the force employed was not very

[29] *Ibid.*, p. 1,140.   [30] *Ibid.*, p. 1,140.

large the purpose above mentioned and the result if the attack had been successful are sufficient in the opinion of the tribunal to justify describing the hostilities as a war. . . . Furthermore . . . the operations of the Japanese troops were, in the opinion of the tribunal, clearly aggressive."[31]

The Nomonhan incident was much larger. It lasted for five months in the summer of 1939; it covered a front of fifty to sixty kilometers in length; and it involved Japanese casualties and prisoners of war totalling—so the majority judgment found—some 50,000 men. It too ended in Japanese defeat. The tribunal concluded: "As in the case of the Lake Khassan Incident the Japanese troops were completely defeated; what would have followed if they had been successful is purely speculative. However, the mere fact that they were defeated does not determine the character of the operations. . . . The tribunal holds that the operations amounted to an aggressive war waged by the Japanese."[32] In his dissent Justice Pal disagreed. "The border incidents," he wrote in his sole reference to either incident, ". . . are mere border incidents."[33]

Having found the Japanese guilty on two counts of aggression, the tribunal still had to deal with a considerable obstacle. Both incidents had ended in negotiated settlements between the Soviet Union and Japan: the agreements of June 9 and August 19, 1940. Further, the two parties concluded a non-aggression pact in the following year. If the parties to the incidents had settled these matters between themselves, how could the Tokyo tribunal reopen them? The majority judgment spoke in these words:

[31] *Ibid.*, p. 834.   [32] *Ibid.*, p. 840.
[33] Pal, *Judgment*, p. 461; see also Röling, "Opinion," pp. 90-93.

138

"In none of the three agreements . . . was any immunity granted nor was the question of liability, criminal or otherwise, dealt with. The tribunal is therefore of the opinion that these agreements afford no defense to the criminal proceedings being taken before this International Tribunal. In a matter of criminal liability whether domestic or international it would be against the public interest for any tribunal to countenance condonation of crime either expressly or by implication."[34]

The international community, the reasoning must have been, has an interest in any bilateral accord that takes precedence over the interests of the immediate parties to that accord.[35] The Soviet Union and Japan reconciled their differences, but that did not close the matter. In other words, no international treaty that settles a dispute without affixing criminal liability can be considered final. Very few important international agreements could stand that test; but the tribunal's position made it possible to reopen in 1946 issues settled in 1938 and 1940. We cannot know whether at Tokyo the Soviet Union took the lead in including these incidents in the indictment. We do know that the Soviet Union forced the indictment of two Japanese officials of importance in Japan's relations with the Soviet Union. We do know that in August 1945 the Soviet Union abrogated unilaterally its Neutrality Pact with

[34] *Judgment*, p. 841.

[35] This was the reasoning of Justice Bernard. "Dissenting Judgment," p. 11. See also President Webb's comment in holding that the *Panay* incident, settled between Japan and the United States, was admissible evidence: "America is one nation; here there are eleven" (*Proceedings*, p. 3,516). Webb remarked later (*Proceedings*, p. 7,786): ". . . if an aggressive war is an offense against international law, no one nation can pardon that offense."

Japan and had attacked its former treaty partner. The majority judgment found the Japanese guilty of aggression against the Soviet Union. It did not consider Soviet acts against Japan.

3. The Axis Alliance

Count 5 of the indictment charged a conspiracy whose object was that ". . . Germany, Italy, and Japan should secure the military, naval, political and economic domination of the whole world. . . ."[36] Chief evidence of the existence of this conspiracy was the Axis alliance, the Tripartite Pact signed by Germany, Italy, and Japan on September 27, 1940. The tribunal held that this count had not been proved. Its verdict read: "We are of opinion that although some of the conspirators clearly desired the achievement of these grandiose objects, nevertheless there is not sufficient evidence to justify a finding that the conspiracy charged in Count 5 has been proved."[37]

However, this failure to convict the Japanese leaders on Count 5 did not prevent the majority from dealing with the Axis alliance at length in its findings on issues of fact. There the majority found the Axis alliance to be ". . . a compact made between aggressor nations for the furtherance of their aggressive purposes."[38] In explanation the majority stated: "The Tripartite Alliance was concluded as a necessary step in Japanese preparations for a military advance into South-East Asia and the South Seas. At the numerous discussions and conferences of September 1940 it was recognized by all who took part that the conclusion of the alliance would commit Japan to waging war against

[36] "Trial of Japanese War Criminals," p. 49.
[37] *Judgment*, p. 1,143.   [38] *Ibid.*, p. 519.

France, the Netherlands, and the countries of the British Commonwealth; and that it implied also Japan's willingness to wage war against the United States, should that country seek to stand between Japan and the attainment of her aggressive aims."[39]

The judgment went on to argue that once the Axis alliance was signed, "active cooperation" took place between Japan and Germany and Italy. Further, the judgment held that the Axis alliance was aimed at the Soviet Union,[40] in spite of three important facts: that Article V of the alliance specifically exempted the Soviet Union; that Japan and the Soviet Union later signed a non-aggression pact; and that Japan did not attack the Soviet Union in spite of German urging.[41]

These findings on issues of fact to the contrary notwithstanding, the tribunal did not find the Japanese leaders guilty on Count 5. There was not "sufficient evidence." But surely if there was sufficient evidence to support these findings of fact, there was sufficient evidence also to convict. This disparity between sections of the judgment is eloquent testimony in support of the objection of the French justice. Justice Bernard decried the fact that the findings on issues of fact had been drawn up by a drafting committee and never submitted to the oral discussion of the full panel of justices.[42]

[39] *Ibid.*, p. 517.   [40] *Ibid.*, p. 823.
[41] Schroeder, *Axis Alliance*, pp. 221-222.
[42] Justice Röling ("Opinion," p. 187) pointed out a second contradiction between the findings of fact and the verdict. In regard to the role of defendant Hata in the fall of the Yonai cabinet, the findings of fact stated that Hata "is not shown to have taken any active part in the plotting which led to the Yonai Cabinet's downfall" (*Judgment*, p. 474). The verdict for Hata read: ". . . in col-

American historians of the Axis alliance have arrived at conclusions far different from those of the majority judgment. Take first Japan's motivation. The Japanese Government signed the pact for many reasons: her diplomatic isolation; her hope of using German good offices with China; her desire to apply diplomatic pressure on the Soviet Union and the United States. "Conspicuous by its absence," writes Paul W. Schroeder, "was a real desire to help the Axis as such."[43] No mention of these "legitimate" motives can be found in the majority judgment. Yet the majority could not claim ignorance of them. As Schroeder writes: ". . . it is exactly these hopes and desires, however illusory, which appear most frequently and prominently in the various discussions and conferences referred to [in the majority judgment]."[44]

Consider next the actual performance of Japan and Germany once the pact was signed. Writes Schroeder: "Only a short time after the signing of the pact, Japanese disappointment with it set in. . . ."[45] Writes Johanna M. Meskill: ". . . in the crucial area of political and military coordination the alliance was ineffective from the start."[46]

---

laboration with and after consulting other high military authorities he precipitated the fall of the Yonai Cabinet . . ." (*Judgment*, p. 1,154). Röling also pointed to a contradiction between the findings of fact and the trial record. The majority had Hata "recommending [Tojo] secretly to the Emperor" (*Judgment*, p. 479). But the language monitor at the trial had ruled "secretly" an incorrect translation, replacing it with "informally" (*Proceedings*, p. 36,610; cited in Röling, "Opinion," p. 186).

[43] Schroeder, *Axis Alliance*, pp. 221, 124-125.

[44] *Ibid.*, p. 221.   [45] *Ibid.*, p. 126.

[46] Johanna Menzel Meskill, *Hitler and Japan: The Hollow Alliance* (New York: Atherton Press, 1966), p. 4.

The Japanese resisted German calls for a Japanese offensive in Southeast Asia in early 1941; the Germans did not tell the Japanese of the impending attack on the Soviet Union (even though the Japanese foreign minister was in Berlin at the end of March 1941); the Japanese went ahead against German warnings to sign their non-aggression pact with the Soviet Union in April; and the Japanese were ready to back away from the alliance in order to facilitate an understanding with the United States during the long negotiations of 1941.[47] So much for the "active cooperation" the majority judgment found.

Schroeder compares the Tokyo judgment's interpretation of the alliance with that of the American Government in 1941. He writes: "It might be noted, first of all, that the position of the tribunal in judging these issues was much different from that of the administration in Washington in 1941. In the latter case, the uncertainty of the evidence, the pressure of events, and the climate of opinion combined to make policy making extremely difficult. If the policy pursued in the latter half of 1941 was a mistake [Schroeder argues that it was], it was certainly only that and, in view of the conditions, an entirely understandable and almost inevitable one. On the other hand, a judicial tribunal, presumably impartial, having a wealth of evidence at hand, under no pressure of time, and dealing with events lying some distance in the past, would clearly be in a better position to judge the issues at stake. In the writer's opinion, the tribunal's decisions of 1948 turned out to be as one-sided and as untenable as those of 1941, and with less reason."

The judgment's account of the alliance, its motivations

---

[47] Schroeder, *Axis Alliance*, Ch. vi; Meskill, *Hitler and Japan.*

and its performance, Schroeder castigates as "wholly misleading."[48]

As Schroeder suggests, there can be scant excuse for the tribunal's findings of fact about the Axis alliance. Certainly the tribunal cannot plead ignorance. If ignorance is precluded, and if we grant the justices a minimal intelligence, then the only explanation must lie in some form of bias: either a will to believe the fundamental outlines of Allied wartime propaganda in the face of the evidence; or a fundamental commitment to the concept of crimes against peace and an unwillingness to admit the unsuitability of that concept to the events preceding the Pacific war.

4. Pearl Harbor

Count 29 of the indictment charged the Japanese leaders with waging "a war of aggression and a war in violation of international law, treaties, agreements, and assurances, against the United States of America" beginning December 7, 1941, the date of the Japanese surprise attack on Pearl Harbor.[49] The majority judgment held that the charge had been proved: "After prolonged negotiations with the United States of America, in which they refused to disgorge any substantial part of the fruits they had seized as the result of their war of aggression against China, on 7th December 1941 the conspirators launched a war of aggression against the United States and the British Commonwealth."[50] Eighteen of the twenty-five accused were found guilty on this count.

[48] Schroeder, *Axis Alliance*, p. 219.
[49] "Trial of Japanese War Criminals," p. 54.
[50] *Judgment*, p. 1,141.

In his opening statement Chief Prosecutor Keenan had sought to condemn the attack on Pearl Harbor for its "stealth, deception, and treachery."[51] After all, American propaganda during the war had focused on the manner of the attack.[52] But nowhere in the majority judgment is there a condemnation of that manner. Instead, the tribunal found the aggressive character of the war to be the primary consideration. Having found the accused guilty of waging a war of aggression, the tribunal felt it unnecessary to establish whether the initiation of that war was in violation of "international law, treaties, agreements and assurances."[53] Among those treaties was Hague Convention III (1907), which in the tribunal's words "... undoubtedly imposes the obligation of giving previous and explicit

[51] "Trial of Japanese War Criminals," p. 27.

[52] Consider this comment of Joseph B. Keenan: "It was our purpose in the beginning to base the prosecution solely on the Pearl Harbor episode and the events immediately contributing thereto. As our study progressed, it became apparent that the defenses of encirclement and self-defense would be asserted. We concluded, and I think correctly so, that it would be necessary at some stage of the trial to develop fully the entire Japanese plan for military aggression, for only by a correct analysis of its origin and purposes could the Japanese situation be pictured in its true light." Quoted by Hanson W. Baldwin, *New York Times*, Dec. 4, 1946, p. 36.

General MacArthur was among those who favored restricting the charge against the Japanese leaders to the sneak attack on Pearl Harbor. But to do so in the face of the Nuremberg precedent was hardly practicable. As Justice Röling wrote in 1960: "The American urge to organize a big trial against Japan was intrinsically based on Pearl Harbor. Since, however, the precedent of Nuremberg was set, it was hardly possible to avoid prosecuting Japanese leaders for the crime against peace. Restricting the Japanese indictment to the undeclared attack on Pearl Harbor would have amounted to a repudiation of the Nuremberg principles." Röling, "Tokyo Trial in Retrospect," p. 256.

[53] *Judgment*, p. 1,144.

145

warning before hostilities are commenced. . . ."[54] The judgment criticized this convention for not being explicit about a minimal period of notice: "It permits of a narrow construction and tempts the unprincipled to try to comply with the obligation thus narrowly construed while at the same time ensuring that their attacks shall come as a surprise. With the margin thus reduced for the purpose of surprise no allowance can be made for error, mishap, or negligence leading to delay in the delivery of the warning, and the possibility is high that the prior warning which the Convention makes obligatory will not in fact be given."[55]

The majority judgment found that the Japanese leaders meant to limit the period of notice to twenty minutes, a period within the strict letter of the Convention. It was not their intent to circumvent Hague Convention III. Rather, it was the lack of "margin for contingencies"[56] that delayed the declaration of war past the actual attack.

Thus, the judgment found the Japanese leaders guilty of aggression against the United States not because of the manner in which that war was begun, but because the war that began with Pearl Harbor was an aggression on the part of the Japanese. Nor was the fact that Japan attacked first a factor of real consequence to the tribunal. After all, the Netherlands declared war on Japan before the Japanese attack on Dutch territory, and yet Japan, not the Netherlands, was held to be the aggressor. The majority judgment explained why: "The fact that the Netherlands, being fully apprised of the imminence of the attack, in self-defense declared war against Japan on 8th December and thus officially recognized the existence of a state

[54] *Ibid.*, p. 986.   [55] *Ibid.*, pp. 988-989.   [56] *Ibid.*, p. 988.

146

of war which had been begun by Japan cannot change that war from a war of aggression on the part of Japan into something other than that."[57] The Japanese Government declared war on the Netherlands more than a month later, on January 11, 1942, the day of the attack on the Dutch East Indies. So much for Robert H. Jackson's emphasis on priority of declaration or attack as the sole criterion of aggression.

The character of the war, not the manner of its inception, was crucial. That character was aggressive: "The tribunal is further of opinion that the attacks which Japan launched on 7th December 1941 against Britain, the United States of America, and the Netherlands were wars of aggression. They were unprovoked attacks, prompted by the desire to seize the possessions of these nations. Whatever may be the difficulty of stating a comprehensive definition of 'a war of aggression,' attacks made with the above motive cannot but be characterized as wars of aggression."[58]

The defense had argued that Japan had been the victim of encirclement, that Japan had gone to war in self-defense. Not so, the majority judgment held: "The measures which were taken by these Powers to restrict Japanese trade were taken in an entirely justifiable attempt to induce Japan to depart from a course of aggression on which she had long been embarked and upon which she had determined to continue. . . . The argument [that Japan acted in self-defense] is indeed merely a repetition of Japanese propaganda issued at the time she was preparing for her wars of aggression. It is not easy to have patience with its lengthy repetition at this date when docu-

[57] *Ibid.*, p. 995. [58] *Ibid.*, p. 994.

147

ments are at length available which demonstrate that Japan's decision to expand to the North, to the West and to the South at the expense of her neighbors was taken long before any economic measures were directed against her and was never departed from."[59]

So much for the appeal to self-defense. It is indeed ironic that the perspective of history gives to the majority judgment precisely the character which that judgment attributed to the attempt to justify Japan's actions as self-defense. The majority judgment is indeed merely a repetition of Allied propaganda issued during the war; and it is not easy to have patience with its lengthy repetition when documents were available to the tribunal which demonstrated its falsity.

Paul W. Schroeder has criticized the majority judgment's interpretation of relations between Japan and America on three major points. First, he asserts, the judgment ". . . traces . . . a firm decision on the part of Japan to attack Pearl Harbor back to April 1941. . . ."[60] This the majority judgment does not do. Although occasional passages (for example, the description of the July 2 decision quoted by Schroeder) and headings (for example, *Decision for War—12 October 1941*) do give a biased and misleading account, the majority judgment taken as a whole makes clear that the final, irreversible decision for war came not in April 1941 but in late November and early December 1941.

Schroeder's second point is that the majority judgment mistakenly concludes ". . . that the whole process of Japanese negotiation was designed solely to deceive."[61] This

[59] *Ibid.*, pp. 991-992.
[60] Schroeder, *Axis Alliance*, p. 223.   [61] *Ibid.*, p. 225.

148

had been the prosecution's contention. But here again Schroeder is misreading the record. The majority judgment does question Japan's willingness ever to yield to Secretary Hull's four principles, but it speculates that Japan hoped the United States could be persuaded through negotiations to "relax the application" of those principles. There is one reference in the majority judgment to the talks "as a screen," but it refers to the period after November 27.[62]

Schroeder's third point is less vulnerable. He argues that the majority judgment misuses evidence. As an example, he cites Prime Minister Konoe's letter of resignation of October 1941, adduced by the majority as evidence that Konoe was committed to a southern advance. Schroeder argues that Konoe was not committed at all. He writes: "A more complete perversion of the Konoe letter and of his entire position can hardly be imagined. . . . The implication thus made by the tribunal . . . is totally untrue."[63]

Without considering further the tribunal's misuse of evidence, let us turn now to two basic issues concerning the Japanese attack on Pearl Harbor: first, the argument that Japan acted in self-defense; second, the issue of American neutrality prior to Pearl Harbor. Our purpose in the following discussion is not to attempt to settle these issues once for all, but to indicate in broad terms the large room for disagreement with the tribunal's majority judgment.

A. THE ISSUE OF SELF-DEFENSE

The general outlines of the argument that Japan acted in self-defense are easily sketched. The argument involves

---

[62] *Judgment*, p. 978; see also p. 974.
[63] Schroeder, *Axis Alliance*, p. 223.

four aspects. The first is the failure of the diplomacy of the 1920's to protect Japanese interests in China and Manchuria in the face of the rising tide of Chinese nationalism. At the Washington Conference of 1922-1923 Japan had traded in her alliance with Great Britain, an alliance on which she could depend, for a multilateral accord upon which she could not depend. With no stable alliance, and with no satisfactory framework of diplomacy in East Asia, Japan inevitably began to think in terms of going it alone. The critical decisions in this direction came in the early 1930's.[64]

The second aspect is an economic one: discrimination against Japanese exports in the years after the Great Depression. The British empire ratified a system of imperial preference at the Ottawa Conference of 1932.[65] The United States, although moving in the 1930's from protectionism to liberal trade policies, discriminated against Japanese products, for example in the Anglo-American agreement of 1938.[66] In his radical critique of American policy toward Japan in the 1930's, the linguist Noam Chomsky has asserted the importance to Japan of such developments. He writes:

"Japan did not have the resiliency to absorb such a serious shock to its economy. The textile industry, which was hit most severely by the discriminatory policies of the

[64] Iriye, *After Imperialism*; Crowley, *Japan's Quest for Autonomy*.

[65] Research Staff, National Institute of Economic and Social Research, ed., *Trade Regulations and Commercial Policy of the United Kingdom* (Cambridge [England]: Cambridge University Press, 1943), pp. 26-27, 170-172.

[66] Carl Kreider, *The Anglo-American Trade Agreement* (Princeton: Princeton University Press, 1943), pp. 212-214.

major imperialist powers, produced nearly half of the total value of manufactured goods and about two thirds of the value of Japanese exports, and employed about half of the factory workers. Though industrialized by Asian standards, Japan had only about one seventh the energy capacity per capita of Germany; from 1927 to 1932, its pig-iron production was 44 percent that of Luxemburg and its steel production about 95 percent. It was in no position to tolerate a situation in which India, Malaya, Indochina, and the Philippines erected tariff barriers favoring the mother country, and could not survive the deterioration in its very substantial trade with the United States and the sharp decline in the China trade. It was, in fact, being suffocated by the American and British and other Western imperial systems, which quickly abandoned their lofty liberal rhetoric as soon as the shoe began to pinch."[67]

In this situation, the argument goes, Japan was forced to establish her own empire.[68]

The third aspect concerns the measures taken by the United States in 1940 and 1941 when Europe was already at war and the situation in the Pacific was deteriorating.

[67] Noam Chomsky, *American Power and the New Mandarins* (New York: Pantheon, 1969), pp. 191-192.

[68] For an opposing view see G. C. Allen, *Short Economic History of Modern Japan* (New York: Praeger, 1963), pp. 159-160: "Apologists for Japan's aggression in China were at one time inclined to argue that her policy was wholly, or mainly, the result of her reaction to the barriers that were being erected against her commercial expansion. This is greatly to overstate the case. The root of Japanese imperialism is certainly not to be found in economic causes. But the circumstances just described no doubt contributed in some measure to the success of the extremists in gaining support for their policies." See also the same author's *Japan's Economic Recovery* (London: Oxford University Press, 1958), especially pp. 9-10, 163-165.

First came the embargo of July 1940 on aviation fuel. September 1940 saw the total embargo on scrap iron. In July 1941 the United States froze all Japanese assets in this country. In August the United States imposed a total embargo on oil. The cumulative effect of these measures was overwhelming. In Schroeder's words: "Through the freezing orders, Japan was denied access to all the vitally needed supplies outside her own control, in particular her most crucial need, oil. The *New York Times* described the order as the most severe blow to Japan possible short of actual war."[69]

These are the measures described by the Tokyo judgment as "an entirely justifiable attempt to induce Japan" to change her policy. But it is clear that these measures were a clear and potent threat to Japan's very existence. The acting Assistant Chief of Staff of the Army Intelligence Service, in arguing for the embargo, stated: "The United States today is in a position to wreck completely the economic structure of the Japanese Empire."[70] For this reason Schroeder suggests that perhaps these measures were ill-chosen; he writes: "The moment that Japan began to draw back, the very force being exerted against her, unless relaxed, would automatically carry the United States to the offense. The measures designed to restrain Japan would serve equally well to force her back."[71]

The fourth aspect is the American posture in the long negotiations of 1941. Schroeder's study of the negotiations indicates that the American stance during 1941 was not a reasonable or even rational one. In particular, the attitude of Secretary of State Hull was hardly conducive to prog-

---

[69] Schroeder, *Axis Alliance*, p. 53.
[70] Quoted in *ibid.*, p. 53.   [71] *Ibid.*, p. 182.

ress. His statement of October 2 poured cold water on the Japanese proposal for a meeting between Prime Minister Konoe and President Roosevelt and generally stiffened the American position. It led Justice Pal to comment: ". . . the position now taken was not quite consistent with the position hitherto assumed for the purpose of the negotiation. The available evidence makes it questionable whether thenceforward the State Department did really negotiate on the question at all; further Japanese efforts thereafter were given scant consideration. Tokyo, it seems, came gradually to feel a lack of sincerity in the American attitude."[72]

The final hardening of American terms came in November, and Justice Pal placed particular weight on Secretary Hull's note of November 26. Pal quoted with approval Charles A. Beard's comment that no one, particularly not President Roosevelt or Secretary Hull, could have been unaware ". . . that the delivery of the document to Japan would prove to be otherwise than a prelude to war."[73]

Schroeder suggests that this hardening of terms—it included resurrecting the spectre of the Axis alliance—was the result of the American estimate that the talks would not bring agreement. He speculates: "The Tripartite Pact was revived as an issue by the American diplomats because it was expected to be useful in selling the anticipated war with Japan to the American people."[74] Schroeder's case is a strong one. It includes a statement by Secretary Hull at

[72] Pal, *Dissent*, p. 531.
[73] Charles A. Beard, *President Roosevelt and the Coming of the War, 1941* (New Haven: Yale University Press, 1948), p. 240; quoted in Pal, *Judgment*, p. 546.
[74] Schroeder, *Axis Alliance*, p. 100.

a White House Conference of November 25. The question was how best to sell a war with Japan to the American people. Writes Schroeder: "Hull contended that a war with Japan should be justified not on the ground of Japanese aggression in Asia, but on the broad grounds of freedom of the seas and 'the fact that Japan was in alliance with Hitler and was carrying out his policies of world aggression.' "[75]

For all his evidence, Schroeder refrains from accusing Secretary Hull of bad faith in his negotiations with the Japanese. He writes: "This is not to say that American leaders, particularly Hull, meant to deceive the American people. One may suppose that Hull really believed that the pact was all that he said it was. It is very easy to believe the worst of one's enemies, particularly when a conflict seems inevitable or is already underway. The only contention here is that Hull found it easy to accept this idea and to pass by a large body of evidence making it dubious, because it fitted the requirements of the situation."[76]

Schroeder reserves his criticism for the Tokyo judgment which, seven years later and in possession of all the evidence, repeated the errors of Secretary Hull. But he affirms that the American position hardened greatly in November. Of the November 26 note he writes: "At one stroke, in prospect of American goods and dollars, Japan was to be changed from a hostile expansionist empire, with great pride in its destiny and ambitious plans for its future, to a peaceful, contented nation of merchants subcontracting with the United States to aid America's fight against Hitler."[77] That this note demanded the renunciation of

[75] *Ibid.*, p. 102.   [76] *Ibid.*, pp. 104-105.   [77] *Ibid.*, pp. 86-87.

the Axis alliance, from which Japan was willing to move away in fact though not ready to renounce in public, is only one of the reasons Schroeder describes it as "incredibly naive."[78]

These four aspects of Japan's relations with the United States are the pillars of the argument that Japan acted in self-defense, resorting to war only under severe economic pressure and even then only after exhausting the possibilities of a negotiated settlement. As Justice Pal commented: "If the negotiation can be taken as contrived by any of the parties only for the purpose of taking time for preparation, then it must be said that such time was not with Japan but with America. Remembering their respective resources, Japan was not to gain anything by lapse of time."[79]

Historians may differ on the relative importance of American and Japanese actions in bringing on the Pacific war, but no historian can deny—as did the majority judgment—that considerations of self-defense played an important role in Japan's actions throughout the prewar period. Miscalculations there may have been on Japan's part; blunders, yes; but not a conspiracy dating from 1928 to wage aggressive war against the United States and its allies.

B. AMERICAN NEUTRALITY

The charge that Japan was the aggressor against the United States at Pearl Harbor and thereafter rests in part at least on the assumption that prior to December 7, 1941 the two nations were at peace. Only if relations prior to

[78] *Ibid.*, p. 86. [79] Pal, *Dissent*, p. 513.

Pearl Harbor were formally proper and peaceful, even if strained, could aggression be charged against the Japanese beginning on December 7. But was this the case?

Justice Pal argued persuasively that it was not. His argument was based on two points. His first was that a state of hostility existed between Japan and China beginning at the latest with the incident at the Marco Polo bridge on July 7, 1937.[80] This date is for him the beginning of the Pacific war, the date from which Japanese actions became subject to the jurisdiction of the Tokyo tribunal. To be sure, neither Japan nor China (nor the United States) formally recognized that a state of war existed; but their failure to do so arose from a mutual interest in circumventing the legal consequences of such recognition, not from any doubt that a war was going on.[81] Further, the Allies at Tokyo indicted the Japanese leaders for aggression in China beginning not in December 1941, not in July 1937, but in September 1931.[82] If Japan stood accused of aggression against China for its actions in 1931 and 1937, then the Allies could hardly argue that no state of war existed in 1937. As Justice Pal wrote: ". . . the Prosecution may not be allowed to characterize this hostility as war for one purpose and not war for the purpose of justifying the United States' action in relation to it."[83] Thus, a state of war between China and Japan existed from July 7, 1937.

Justice Pal's second point is that if a state of war existed between Japan and China, then the United States was

[80] *Ibid.*, p. 580.   [81] *Ibid.*, pp. 580-582.

[82] Count 18 of the indictment, "Trial of Japanese War Criminals," p. 52.

[83] Pal, *Dissent*, p. 548.

156

bound by international law either to enter the war or to stay out. The United States, however, tried to have it both ways. While formally ignoring the state of war that existed, the United States nevertheless took many steps intended to aid China in its fight against Japan. These steps included the economic measures discussed above, and several other steps: the moral embargo of July 1938 against the export of aircraft to Japan; the denunciation in July 1939 of the commercial treaty of 1911; the appointment in June 1941 of an American political advisor to Chiang Kai-shek; the permission for General Chennault and his flyers to resign from the American armed forces and volunteer for duty with the Chinese; and the appointment of a military mission to China in August 1941.[84] With these steps, argued Justice Pal, the United States became a party to the conflict, not an innocent and neutral bystander. Wrote Pal: ". . . the employment of measures like those taken by the Allied nations against Japan, then engaged in war with China, amounted to a direct participation in the conflict. Their conduct was in defiance of the theory of neutrality and of the fundamental obligations that the law of nations still imposes upon non-belligerent Powers. . . . Justly or unjustly, rightly or wrongly, the Allied Nations had already participated in the conflict by these actions and any hostile measures taken against them by Japan *thereafter* would not be 'aggressive.' "[85]

Hence, Japan's attack on Pearl Harbor and subsequent warfare against the United States constituted a legitimate response to the measures that the United States had already taken. In Justice Pal's words: "Here, at this stage, we are only concerned with the question as to how to view

[84] *Ibid.*, p. 548.   [85] *Ibid.*, pp. 553-554.

the action taken by the United States in helping China against Japan. If it was an act of belligerency, it does not matter whether it was aggressive or defensive; the two countries would no longer, in the eye of law, be at peace. It was not an act of belligerency only if there was no war between China and Japan."[86]

By this argument Japan was not guilty of aggression against the United States. Japan might have been guilty of aggression against China, although Justice Pal argued that she was not;[87] but even conceding Japanese aggression against China, Japan could not be guilty of the same charge against the United States. Justice Pal concluded: "The evidence does not entitle us to characterize the Japanese attack as a sudden, unexpected, treacherous act committed while relations between the two countries were peaceful."[88]

Japan did attack the United States at Pearl Harbor. That attack did mark the opening of the shooting war in the Pacific. But Japan was moved in significant measure by considerations of self-defense, and the attack was not without provocation.

The Tokyo Tribunal failed miserably in its attempt to write the history of the prewar years. This failure was in part the result of the tribunal's bias, but it was also in large part the result of the fundamental misconceptions that lay behind the trial and dominated its course. The indictment and the judgment assumed that Japanese history could be explained in terms of a conspiracy, and that that conspiracy was bent on aggression. An unbiased look at the evidence would have forced drastic revision of both these misconceptions. But an unbiased approach to the

[86] *Ibid.*, p. 548. [87] *Ibid.*, p. 562. [88] *Ibid.*, p. 554.

evidence: this the tribunal was not prepared to undertake. Reflecting on the Tokyo Tribunal's mistakes, Schroeder concludes with a statement no historian will challenge: ". . . the processes of history are too complex to be subjected to the adjudication of a military tribunal."[89] But surely we must go one step further and conclude that the processes of history are too complex to be subjected to the adjudication of *any* tribunal. Historical process does not yield to adjudication; and the attempt to make history justiciable is doomed from the start. The mistakes of Tokyo were attributable in part to bias and to restrictions on admissible evidence. But the larger share of the blame must fall on the basic misconception that the events at issue could be adjudicated.[90]

[89] Schroeder, *Axis Alliance*, p. 228.

[90] On this point see Julius Stone's comment: "If international judges could be found with supreme skill as historians and supreme objectivity as judges, they might still reconstruct an approximation to the full truth by gathering together, cross-checking, correcting, and re-integrating the dismembered and distorted national versions created and sponsored by interested states. This is conceivable; but only barely so. And it is at least as likely that the several limbs of dismembered Truth will, like those of the hero of the Finnish Kalevala myth, Lemminkäinen, move steadily down the spacious river of fact and fiction on which men drift towards the sea of oblivion. Unlike the fortunate Lemminkäinen, however, our dismembered Truth may have no devoted Mother to stand with infinite patience on the banks, to retrieve the severed members and restore them with loving care to sentient life. The segments which even our ablest historians could retrieve and reconstruct would too often be those, not of Truth itself, but of a robot or a puppet, which 'lives' and 'moves' not by the inspiration of human love, but by the digitated strings of State propaganda." Stone, *Aggression and World Order*, p. 144.

VI.

AFTER THE TRIAL

> . . . the Tokyo and Nuremberg war crimes trials were manifestations of an intellectual and moral revolution which will have a profound and far-reaching influence upon the future of world society.
> —Joseph B. Keenan and Brendan F. Brown, 1950

> It is more and more evident to us that the good name of justice, let alone of the United States, has been compromised . . . in Tokyo.
> —Washington *Post*, Jan. 11, 1949

WE HAVE considered the Tokyo trial from the aspects of international law, of procedure, and of history. In each aspect we have found there to be at least serious question about the integrity of the tribunal and at most compelling evidence that the trial was a biased proceeding. But the trial did not end with the judgment.

1. The Tokyo Trial and General Douglas MacArthur

The Tokyo Charter contained a provision for review by the Supreme Commander for the Allied Powers in Japan, General Douglas MacArthur. What did not appear in the charter was a policy decision of the Far Eastern Commission calling for General MacArthur to consult first with the diplomatic representatives in Japan of the members of the Far Eastern Commission. This policy decision, kept secret through the early stages of the trial,[1] served to deepen the political character of the trial. To an administrative review of a judicial decision it added diplomatic consultations with those nations already represented at the trial by associate prosecutors and justices. The Nuremberg Charter had contained no provision for review.

The defense availed itself of the right of appeal to General MacArthur. Within a week of the sentencing, all defense counsel joined in a single appeal. Part of this appeal, the section dealing with the evils of majority rule among the justices, we have already quoted. The whole statement is included as an appendix. The following is its final paragraph:

"If we hope for a world organized under law and operating under the rule of law and the principles of justice, we must not ourselves be guilty of atrocities against the law and justice. No good, but only pyramided evil, will come from the verdict of this tribunal as it now stands. A fearless act of statesmanship now can salvage much of the prestige which the act of this small group of judges would lose to our countries: we urge that it be performed."[2]

The tribunal had not spoken with one voice. The eleven justices had written six separate opinions. The majority decision was signed by nine of the eleven justices. Three of these nine issued separate opinions, as did the two who refused to sign the majority judgment. The concurring opinion of Justice Jaranilla of the Philippines included the assertion that the majority had disregarded too many counts of the indictment and the complaint that "a

[1] Hankey, *Politics*, p. 122.   [2] See Appendix 4.

few only of the penalties imposed by the tribunal" were "too lenient, not exemplary and deterrent, and not commensurate with the gravity of the offense or offenses committed."[3] At the Nuremberg trial it was the Russian justice who took the hardest line; at Tokyo it was the survivor of the Bataan Death March.

In his concurring statement, President Webb argued that the punishment of death was perhaps not the most appropriate one. If deterrence is "the main purpose of punishment for an offense," argued Webb, then "imprisonment for life under sustained conditions of hardship in an isolated place or places outside Japan . . . would be a greater deterrent to men like the accused than the speedy termination of existence on the scaffold or before a firing squad."[4] Two further considerations supported the commutation of death sentences to life imprisonment. First, the convicted leaders were old and no longer impressive men. Said Webb: "It may prove revolting to hang or shoot such old men." Second, the "leader in the crime, though available for trial, had been granted immunity." Wrote Webb: "Justice requires me to take into consideration the Emperor's immunity when determining the punishment of the accused found guilty."[5]

Justice Bernard of France signed the majority judgment but dissented from it strongly. He believed on natural law grounds that aggressive war constituted a crime and that individuals could be held responsible for acts of state; but he concluded that the procedure of the Tokyo trial had been grossly lacking. He wrote: "Though I am of opinion that the charter permitted granting to the accused guarantees sufficient for their defense, I think that these actually

[3] Jaranilla, "Concurring Opinion," p. 34.
[4] Webb, "Separate Opinion," p. 17.   [5] Ibid., pp. 18, 19.

162

were not granted to them. Essential principles, violation of which would result in most civilized nations in the nullity of the entire procedure, and the right of the tribunal to dismiss the case against the accused, were not respected."[6] Among the defects of procedure were the manner of deliberations among the justices and the failure to indict the emperor. Bernard's conclusion was straightforward: "A verdict reached by a tribunal after a defective procedure cannot be a valid one."[7]

Justice Röling of Holland issued his dissenting opinion for the express purpose of appealing to General MacArthur to reduce several of the sentences. Röling agreed with six of the seven death penalties; but Hirota, he argued, had not been proved guilty of *any* charge. Three defendants should have been condemned to death instead of merely to life imprisonment, but the Supreme Commander, of course, had authority only to reduce sentences. Five men, including Hirota and Shigemitsu, should have been acquitted on all counts.[8] Justice Pal's was the final dissenting opinion. We have seen that he found all defendants innocent on all counts.

In sum, one justice found all defendants innocent. One found all defendants not guilty by reason of defective procedure. One found that Hirota, sentenced to death, and four others sentenced to lesser terms were innocent. One justice spoke out against any death penalties. Six justices spoke only through the majority judgment. And one justice protested the majority judgment's leniency in a few cases.[9] The majority judgment condemned Hirota to

---

[6] Bernard, "Dissenting Judgment," p. 18.

[7] *Ibid.*, p. 20.　　　　　　　　[8] Röling, "Opinion," pp. 178ff.

[9] See Chapter IV, note 43, for Kojima's speculation on how the various judges voted.

death, but three justices found him innocent of all crime and a fourth recommended commutation.

In November 1948 General Douglas MacArthur presided over the fate of the Japanese leaders convicted at the Tokyo trial. Would he uphold the majority judgment? Or would he demonstrate in this field too his strong penchant for independence? Throughout the trial General MacArthur had sought to minimize his involvement in the trial. He appointed the justices, and he would review their judgment. But he had his doubts about the whole thing. Wrote his aide and ardent admirer Major General Courtney Whitney: ". . . the principle of holding criminally responsible the political leaders of the vanquished in war was repugnant to him. He felt that to do so was to violate the most fundamental rules of criminal justice."[10] Moreover, he had a strong sympathy and genuine admiration for the Japanese people. In 1945 he had vehemently opposed the indictment of the emperor. But would all these feelings affect his review?

The Far Eastern Commission in Washington in early 1946 had demanded a voice in the review, but no provision to that effect appeared in the Charter. When the time came for review, that voice was exercised by the Allied Council for Japan, made up of diplomatic representatives of the Allied Powers in Tokyo. The conditions under which the Allied Council met did not make for a meaningful review. The meeting was held on November 24, twelve days after the Tokyo Tribunal had handed down its sentences, and only three days after the defense counsel had filed their petition for review.

Chairman of the Allied Council was the American representative, William J. Sebald. He had proposed to the

[10] Whitney, *MacArthur*, p. 280.

State Department that he "comment" on Justice Webb's "gratuitous and politically damaging opinion on the emperor," but the State Department had said no.[11] Sebald did not refer to the equally damaging comments of Justice Bernard. That he did not is indicative of the haste which such tight scheduling forced upon the reviewing body. The French representative, for example, was unable on November 24 to offer any statement on behalf of his government.

At the meeting General MacArthur called first on Sebald. In Sebald's words: "I was called on first, presumably on the theory that I would set the pattern by being succinct and unequivocal. Loudly and clearly I said: 'I have no change to recommend.' "[12] MacArthur then called upon the other diplomats in alphabetical order by nation. The national stances reflected the opinions of each nation's justice. Perhaps this was the intent of the various foreign ministries; or perhaps it was a reflection of the lack of instructions from the various foreign ministries. Australia held that reduction of sentences was the province of the Supreme Commander. France made no official comment; but the French diplomat, citing Justice Bernard's dissent, made a personal appeal for clemency. India favored commuting all death sentences to life imprisonment "in view of the development of international feeling against the death penalty." The Netherlands recommended commuting Hirota's sentence to life and reducing four other

[11] William J. Sebald with Russell Brines, *With MacArthur in Japan* (New York: Norton, 1965), p. 168. The account in Hankey (*Politics*, pp. 122-123) is largely inaccurate. It includes the charge that some of the dissenting opinions were not yet printed. Defense counsel George A. Furness affirms that all defense counsel had copies of all dissents for use in drawing up their appeals.
[12] *Ibid.*

165

sentences.[13] All seven nations whose justices had constituted the majority—the United States, China, New Zealand, the Philippines, the U.S.S.R., and the United Kingdom—favored no change.

The tribunal's justices had spoken, but with a mixed voice. The Allied nations had spoken, but again with a mixed voice. Now it was up to General MacArthur. His own proclamation, as eloquent as any he wrote, must speak for itself. It is quoted here in its entirety:

"No duty I have ever been called upon to perform in a long, public service replete with many bitter, lonely, and forlorn assignments and responsibilities is so utterly repugnant to me as that of reviewing the sentences of the Japanese war criminal defendants by the International Military Tribunal for the Far East. It is not my purpose, nor indeed would I have that transcendent wisdom which would be necessary, to assay the universal fundamentals involved in these epochal proceedings designed to formulate and codify standards of international morality by those charged with the nation's conduct. The problem indeed is basically one which man has struggled to solve since the beginning of time, and which may well wait complete solution till the end of time.

"Insofar as my own immediate obligation and limited authority in this case is concerned, suffice it that under the principles and procedures described in full detail by the Allied Powers concerned, I can find nothing of commission or omission in the incidents of the trial itself of sufficient import to warrant my intervention in the judgments which have been rendered. No human decision is infalli-

[13] "Proceedings on Review Before General MacArthur," 23 Nov. 1948, pp. 1-2.

ble, but I can conceive of no judicial process where greater safeguard was made to evolve justice.

"It is inevitable that many will disagree with the verdict; even the learned justices who composed the tribunal were not in complete unanimity, but no mortal agency in the present imperfect evolution of civilized society seems more entitled to confidence in the integrity of its solemn pronouncements. If we cannot trust such processes and such men, we can trust nothing. I therefore direct the Commanding General of the Eighth Army to execute the sentences as pronounced by the tribunal. In doing so, I pray that an Omnipotent Providence may use this tragic expiation as a symbol to summon all persons of good will to the realization of the utter futility of war—the most malignant scourge and greatest sin of mankind—and eventually to its renunciation by all nations. To this end, on the day of execution, I request the members of all the congregations throughout Japan of whatever creed or faith in the privacy of their homes or at their altars of public worship to seek divine help and guidance that the world will keep the peace, lest the human race perish."[14]

According to two friendly accounts, those of Major General Whitney and Ambassador Sebald, the decision was not an easy one for General MacArthur. Wrote Sebald: "The General obviously was deeply affected and moved by the decision he had made and which, apparently, I was the first to share with him. I had not seen him display such deep emotion before. In almost a whisper, he said: 'Bill, that was a difficult decision to make.' "[15] There is material, however, to support a less generous in-

[14] Text in Whitney, *MacArthur*, pp. 281-282.
[15] Sebald, *With MacArthur*, p. 170.

terpretation of MacArthur's action. For one thing, General MacArthur had taken steps in January 1946 to preclude an appeal from Tokyo to the U.S. Supreme Court.[16] For another, he engineered the diplomatic consultation to produce a desired result, first by giving very little notice and then by calling on Sebald first to stampede the diplomats. Finally, in spite of judicial and diplomatic excuses for exercising the power of mercy that was his, MacArthur upheld the verdict and the sentences of the Tokyo trial.

It behooves us to consider carefully General MacArthur's reasons for upholding the verdicts. He began, so General Whitney stated, with the conviction that to hold "criminally responsible the political leaders of the vanquished in war" was "to violate the most fundamental rules of criminal justice." Why then did General MacArthur not act on this basic (and, we have argued, correct) premise? There seem to have been three reasons. First, General MacArthur's training was not a legal one, and he had little choice but to put his trust in the justices nominated by the various nations. Second, General MacArthur had time only for the most cursory review of the tribunal's proceedings. Third, General MacArthur operated under a strong impression of the "utter futility of war." Hence he was interested in any gesture that might impress this idea upon the world at large.

We cannot assume that this third motive was the strongest. However, were that the case, it would accord well

[16] *Facts on File*, v (1945) 395J, reported for Dec. 5, 1945 that General MacArthur "revises war-crimes trial procedures, placing defendants under the jurisdiction of the Allies instead of just the U.S. and thus precluding appeals to the U.S. Supreme Court, as in Yamashita's case."

with the sentiments of many people in the immediate postwar world. War was hell, and it brought civilization to the brink of extinction. Something must be done; some gesture had to be made. Punishment should be meted out even where technically no crime had been committed.[17] Only in such an atmosphere do the words of the Nuremberg and Tokyo judgments make sense: ". . . so far from it being unjust to punish him [the attacker], it would be unjust if his wrong were allowed to go unpunished."[18] These were noble sentiments, to be sure. Yet they do not alter the uncomfortable facts. Gross injustice was committed at Tokyo. The leaders of the defeated nation, and they alone, were offered as a sacrifice to a better world. Although wars have continued since 1945, no additional payments (Adolf Eichmann excepted) have been added to these first down-payments on a better world.[19]

2. The Tokyo Trial and the Supreme Court

General MacArthur had kept silent on the legal issues raised by the Tokyo trial. The failure to face these legal issues continued when certain of the defendants lodged an

[17] For example, see the two essays by Charles E. Wyzanski, Jr., reprinted in his *Whereas—a Judge's Premises* (Boston: Little, Brown, 1965). The first is a strong attack on the Nuremberg trial; the second is a much less convincing recantation.

[18] *Nuremberg Judgment*, I, 219; quoted in *Tokyo Judgment*, p. 26.

[19] See Morton A. Kaplan and Nicholas deB. Katzenbach, *The Political Foundations of International Law* (New York: Wiley, 1961), pp. 45-46: "To make sense, these tribunals [the Nuremberg trials] had to represent a development toward an ordered world community in which the use of force by national authorities without sanction from some international body was outlawed and in which effective tribunals for punishing transgressors were established. . . ."

appeal with the Supreme Court of the United States for writs of habeas corpus. The Court first voted five to four to hear preliminary arguments (four of the justices were already convinced that the Court lacked jurisdiction). To his credit, Robert H. Jackson voted in favor of hearing preliminary arguments, thus breaking a tie.[20] But on December 20, 1948, the Court made its decision:

"1. The military tribunal set up in Japan by General MacArthur as the agent of the Allied Powers is not a tribunal of the United States and the courts of the United States have no power or authority to review, affirm, set aside, or annul the judgments and sentences imposed by it on these petitioners, all of whom are residents and citizens of Japan.

"2. For this reason, their motions for leave to file petitions for writs of habeas corpus are denied."[21]

Justice Jackson abstained. Justice Rutledge reserved his opinion but failed to state it before his death in 1949. Justice Murphy dissented without recording his reasons.

In a concurring opinion, Justice Douglas attacked the narrowness of the criterion of jurisdiction advanced by the Supreme Court's majority. That formula, wrote Justice Douglas, is ". . . indeed potentially dangerous. It leaves practically no room for judicial scrutiny of this new type of military tribunal. . . . It leaves the power of those tribunals absolute. Prisoners held under its mandates may have appeal to the conscience or mercy of an executive; but they apparently have no appeal to law. . . . I cannot believe

---

[20] See his memorandum, 335 *U.S. Reports*, 876-881 (Dec. 6, 1948).

[21] 338 *U.S. Reports*, 197 (June 27, 1949).

that we would adhere to that formula if these petitioners were American citizens."[22]

Why then did Justice Douglas agree that the Supreme Court lacked jurisdiction? Because he found the Tokyo trial to be a political forum, not a judicial action. He wrote: "The conclusion is therefore plain that the Tokyo Tribunal acted as an instrument of military power of the Executive Branch of government. It responded to the will of the Supreme Commander as expressed in the military order by which he constituted it. It took its law from its creator and did not act as a free and independent tribunal to adjudge the rights of petitioners under international law. As Justice Pal said, it did not therefore sit as a judicial tribunal. It was solely an instrument of political power. Insofar as American participation is concerned, there is no constitutional objection to that action. For the capture and control of those who were responsible for the Pearl Harbor incident was a political question on which the President as Commander-in-Chief, and as spokesman for the nation in foreign affairs, had the final say."[23]

The Tokyo trial, Justice Douglas argued, "took its law from its creator and did not act as a free and independent tribunal"; the Tokyo trial was "solely an instrument of political power." Justice Douglas' opinion confirms much of what we have argued about the Tokyo trial. It is of great use to critics of the trial; but it was of no use whatsoever to the defendants. For one thing, it concurred with the finding that the U.S. Supreme Court had no jurisdiction. For another, it was not submitted until June 1949,

[22] 338 *U.S. Reports*, 203-204, 205 (June 27, 1949).
[23] 338 *U.S. Reports*, 215 (June 27, 1949).

six months after the execution of the seven defendants condemned to die.

3. The Prisoners

Seven men, including Tojo Hideki and Hirota Koki, were hanged on December 23, 1948. A vote of six to five had determined the method of their execution, an ignominious one. The clothing prescribed by their jailers for the execution was a further humiliation. They were not permitted to wear their old uniforms or even civilian clothing of their own choosing. Instead, they went to their deaths wearing "United States army salvage work clothing completely devoid of insignia of any kind."[24] Eighteen men received sentences of imprisonment, sixteen of them for life. Six of these men died in prison. The other twelve served only part of their sentences.

The Charter had given the Supreme Commander of the Allied Powers the authority to reduce the sentences "at any time." In addition, a special SCAP directive had been issued on March 7, 1950. It authorized the reduction of sentences by two thirds for good behavior and parole after fifteen years for prisoners with sentences of life imprisonment.[25] But not until two full years after the end of the Tokyo trial and eight months after the parole provision had been instituted did General MacArthur see fit to act. And only in one case did he act at all.

Former Foreign Minister Shigemitsu Mamoru walked out of prison on November 21, 1950. He had received the shortest sentence, seven years from date of arraignment.

[24] "Official Report of the Japanese Executions," SCAP Public Relations, *New York Times*, Dec. 23, 1948, p. 6.
[25] *Facts on File*, x (1950), 75N.

By the time of his release he had served four years and seven months of his seven-year sentence. Shigemitsu soon returned to his former pursuits. Only four years later, in December of 1954, Shigemitsu became Foreign Minister once again. During his two years in office he negotiated with John Foster Dulles and other Allied foreign ministers the release of the remaining prisoners of the Tokyo trial.[26]

The Allied Occupation ended in 1952, and with the Occupation terminated also the writ of the Allied Powers in Japan. But the Treaty of Peace with Japan signed at the San Francisco Peace Conference of September 1951 included an article concerning the convicted war criminals. Article 11 read: "Japan accepts the judgments of the International Military Tribunal for the Far East and of other Allied War Crimes Courts both within and outside Japan, and will carry out the sentences imposed thereby upon Japanese nationals imprisoned in Japan. . . . In the case of persons sentenced by the International Military Tribunal for the Far East, such power [to grant clemency, to reduce sentences and to parole] may not be exercised except on the decision of a majority of the governments represented on the tribunal, and on the recommendation of Japan."[27] The political verdicts of the Tokyo trial would be followed by political paroles, reductions of sentences, and clemency.

"Conference" is a misnomer for the San Francisco gathering. It produced signatures on a document, but the terms of that document were not under discussion at the

[26] See, for example, *Facts on File*, xv (1955), 287AB3.

[27] U.S. Department of State, *Conference for the Conclusion and Signature of the Treaty of Peace with Japan*, Department of State Publication 4392 (Washington: U.S. Government Printing Office, 1951), p. 317.

conference. The text of the treaty had been worked out in negotiations among the United States, Great Britain, and Japan. The forty-nine other nations participating at San Francisco had been invited to ratify a "final text" issued almost a month before the conference opened.[28] Article 11 of this "final text" was identical with the same article of the final treaty quoted above.

At the conference only El Salvador and Mexico discussed Article 11 at all. El Salvador pleaded on general humanitarian grounds for "greater latitude for the Japanese Government."[29] Mexico protested against the legal basis of the trial. The Mexican spokesman said: "We would also have desired that the same article not continue legalizing, with reference to the Allied War Crimes Tribunals . . . an attitude which we believe is not completely in harmony with juridical principles and is not in consonance with the best principles of modern civilization which are enumerated in the juridical phrase, *Nullum crimen sine lege, nulla poena sine lege,* a principle which inspires the penal legislation of all cultured peoples of the world. . . ."[30] But the draft treaty was the final treaty, and so no amendment was offered. The Mexican spokesman spoke only for the record.

With the end of the Occupation in 1952, the Japanese Ministry of Justice took over from the U.S. Eighth Army as jailer of the Tokyo prisoners, but the Japanese Government was without authority to alter the sentences imposed in any way.

What criteria guided the Japanese Government in its appeals for parole? The answer is not clear. One report

[28] Department of State, *Treaty of Peace,* pp. 19, 37.
[29] *Ibid.,* p. 140.   [30] *Ibid.,* pp. 98-99.

has health as the major factor in the parole of the first five men.[31] The parole of the final seven prisoners followed soon thereafter. But why should Hashimoto, guilty on two counts, precede Oshima, guilty on one, by three full months? Or why should Sato come last? After all, Kaya, Kido, Hoshino, and Suzuki had all been convicted on the same five counts as Sato. Once again there is reason to suspect political and/or arbitrary handling of the prisoners of the Tokyo trial.

The final act of the saga of the Tokyo trial came on April 7, 1958. On that day the Japanese Foreign Ministry announced the unconditional release of the ten surviving parolees. One account read: "The ten were ordered freed after Japanese Government clemency appeals had been approved by signatories of the 1951 San Francisco peace treaty."[32] Indictment, trial, verdict and sentences, appeal, imprisonment, parole, and now clemency: only the verdict of history was missing.

4. The Tokyo Trial Today

It is perhaps too early to speak of the verdict of history on the Tokyo trial. But surely it is not too early to conclude that the Japanese accused were woefully wronged.[33]

[31] *Kyodo kenkyu: Paru hanketsusho*, ed. Tokyo saiban kenkyu-kai (Tokyo: 1966), p. 85.

[32] *Facts on File*, xviii (1958), 113D2.

[33] In 1950 Chief Prosecutor Keenan published a book entitled *Crimes Against International Law* (with Brendan Francis Brown, Washington: Public Affairs Press), dedicated "to the memory of Francisco Suarez and Hugo Grotius." There, in his extraordinary (and extraordinarily self-serving) final chapter, Keenan plays down the issue of actual guilt or innocence of the Tokyo defendants. Securing their conviction, he writes, was "only passing, ephemeral, transitory, and indeed only momentary." What was important was

175

In that they were leaders of their nation and indicted in effect as representatives of their nation, their nation too was woefully wronged.

The objection may be raised that it is unwise to reopen

the "grander and wider aim of the trial (i.e.) to advance the cause of peace and right notions of international law," to assist "in the creation of a jural situation, which would afford an opportunity for the operation of judging processes to reconstruct international criminal law." Sadly, however, the defense counsel did not share this high goal. To be sure, the purpose of the defense counsel is to defend the accused, and a certain amount of advocacy is to be expected. "But apparently the defense permitted the immediate aim of the acquittal of the defendants to subordinate the greater and ultimate purposes of the case. It was regrettable that the defense should have so over-emphasized the duty of advocacy as to defend the proposition that the great nations were insincere, or even were committing a fraud upon the Family of Nations, when they agreed in written commitments that it was imperative to conform their actions, thenceforth, to ancient notions of right, justice, law, and punishment, grounded on right reason. In order to facilitate the interests of their clients, it seems that the defense were willing to sacrifice the common international good. . . ."

Having established these priorities Keenan looked philosophically upon the possibility that some of the Tokyo defendants had been misjudged. "Had there been an actual miscarriage of justice with regard to some of the defendants, there would have been no wrong. . . . The situation of the defendants was comparable to that of American soldiers about to take a beachhead; that is, the lives of morally and legally innocent men may be sacrificed in the achievement of the ultimate purpose, but the common good requires the taking of the beachhead. The loss of lives is not willed. Every reasonable effort has been made to prevent it" (pp. 155-157). It seems likely, however, that by "morally and legally innocent men" Keenan meant to refer primarily to Shigemitsu Mamoru. There is a letter from Keenan to Shigemitsu's American defense counsel George A. Furness, dated February 9, 1952, in which Keenan expresses his realization that the inclusion of Shigemitsu was an error and his surprise at Shigemitsu's conviction. Unfortunately, the original cannot be found, and only Japanese translations survive.

now an issue that the Japanese people themselves never really protested. They too had a maxim about might making right, and so they were prepared for some irrational vengeance from their conquerors. Nor were they particularly proud of their wartime leaders or sorry to see them punished. Moreover, most Japanese have come to agree at least with the major early aims of the Occupation, and the Tokyo trial is far less important to them than, say, land reform. Finally, there is some danger in denouncing the trial today. Japan today is only just emerging from her postwar political dependence on the United States; and denunciation of the trial may play into the hands of reactionary elements in Japanese politics.

My answer here is twofold. First, I do hold a brief for justice, even to enemies. I do not hold a brief for Tojo Hideki and his fellow defendants at the Tokyo trial. My purpose has been to examine the Tokyo trial—its law, its procedure, and its judgment—and in the course of that examination I have found the Tokyo trial highly defective. But this is not to argue that Japan's prewar policy was faultless, reasonable, or even defensible. Tojo's reputation and the history of the period are involved, but only peripherally. I argue that Tojo and the others were misjudged at the Tokyo trial. But I do not attempt to come to a new historical judgment. There may be little connection between legal guilt and innocence on the one hand and historical verdict on the other.

Second, I am concerned about the whole course of postwar American foreign policy, particularly in Asia and most obviously in Vietnam. I think that many of the ideals and preconceptions that lay behind the Tokyo trial have played a contributing role in the more recent mistakes that

177

the United States has made and continues to make in Asia. Among these preconceptions are the belief that change in the international arena should come only through peaceful means, that resort to force is unjustifiable whatever the provocation, that aggressive war (assuming we can decide what aggression means) is illegal.

Secretary of State Dean Rusk talked endlessly of "aggression." President Nixon speaks of his goal as "a generation of peace." To dismiss these phrases as mere propaganda is to miss the vital point that they really did, and do, hold meaning for the speakers. Is it farfetched to hear in these phrases the strong echo of the Pact of Paris, the London Conference, and the Nuremberg and Tokyo verdicts? I think not. If an examination of the Tokyo trial can contribute to rethinking our more recent assumptions, then that alone is ample justification for this study.

Now that in Vietnam the shoe is on the other foot and serious defense of American policy is very difficult, we may be somewhat more ready than we were before to question the precedents established at Nuremberg and Tokyo. Not only are crimes against peace of a highly political nature, but the conditions of the postwar world are not conducive to fairness. Justice Pal's judgment is evidence that objectivity in the immediate postwar world is not unattainable. But, given the stakes involved and the political nature of the appointment of judges, it is highly unlikely that such objectivity will carry the day. It is also inevitably the case that only defeated leaders risk trial. In the words of Chief Prosecutor Keenan: "The recipe for rabbit stew is first to catch the rabbit."[34]

[34] "Joseph B. Keenan Meets the Press," p. 460.

But what are the alternatives? Do we leave enemy leaders to their national courts for disposition? The experience with Germany after World War I suggests that this course has its defects. So also does the intervention of President Nixon in the case of Lieutenant Calley in 1971.[35] Do we shoot enemy leaders out of hand, as the British Government urged in 1945? No. Surely it is better to hold a trial. Had there been no Tokyo trial, there would be no records, or fewer records, on the basis of which to conclude that the Japanese leaders were condemned unjustly. But there are great disadvantages too, disadvantages arising largely out of self-deception.

The trial was a kind of morality play, a reaffirmation of a world-view that had been one factor in the making of World War II. To the extent that this world-view was itself invalid, the Tokyo trial was harmful rather than helpful. It prolonged our immersion in the unreal world of our

[35] To be sure, Mr. Nixon has yet to exercise the review he promised. However, the circumstances under which he announced his intent to review are portentous. So also are the terms in which Presidential Advisor John D. Ehrlichman described the review: "non-legal and non-technical." The parallel is precise with the original American memorandum on Nuremberg (quoted above on page 17), which inveighed against "technical contentions and legalistic arguments." In both cases the statements are tantamount to admissions that the law as it stands yields unsatisfactory results. It is natural that there should be anguish over the fact that Lieutenant Calley faces punishment and the generals and presidents do not. The remedy here is not clemency for the lieutenants but indictments for the policy-makers, military and civilian. At issue is *not* crimes against peace, *not* the determination that America has committed an aggression; but conventional war crimes, such policies as population transfers and free-fire zones. On this subject see Telford Taylor, *Nuremberg and Vietnam: An American Tragedy* (Chicago: Quadrangle, 1970).

dreams. In this sense, perhaps, summary executions might have been preferable.

However, to limit the options to trial by national courts, summary execution, and international trial à la Tokyo is in itself evidence of political immaturity. It may just be that enemy leaders are sincere men, that the conflict arises not from malevolence but from other less corrigible factors. If that is the case, then there must be a fourth option: no trial at all. Only if that fourth option is strong can there be any real confidence that justice will be served by invocation of the legal process. But in view of the limitations of human nature it would seem wiser simply to oppose from the start the idea of trials after war, except, again, for conventional war crimes. For defeated leaders the fact of defeat itself is surely of greater moment than any subsequent punishment.

We come then to the end of our study of the Tokyo trial. We have examined lofty motives and base motives. We have found its foundation in international law to be shaky. We have seen that its process was seriously flawed. We have examined the verdict's inadequacy as history. "Victors' justice" is a harsh judgment, but a harsh judgment is called for. It is only slight mitigation that in punishing the Japanese leaders we deceived ourselves.

APPENDICES

1.

PROCLAMATION BY THE SUPREME COMMANDER FOR THE ALLIED POWERS, JANUARY 19, 1946

W HEREAS, the United States and the Nations allied therewith in opposing the illegal wars of aggression of the Axis Nations, have from time to time made declarations of their intentions that war criminals should be brought to justice;

Whereas, the Governments of the Allied Powers at war with Japan on the 26th July 1945 at Potsdam, declared as one of the terms of surrender that stern justice shall be meted out to all war criminals including those who have visited cruelties upon our prisoners;

Whereas, by the Instrument of Surrender of Japan executed at Tokyo Bay, Japan, on the 2nd September 1945, the signatories for Japan, by command of and in behalf of the Emperor and the Japanese government, accepted the terms set forth in such Declaration at Potsdam;

Whereas, by such Instrument of Surrender, the authority of the Emperor and the Japanese Government to rule the state of Japan is made subject to the Supreme Commander for the Allied Powers, who is authorized to take such steps as he deems proper to effectuate the terms of surrender;

Whereas, the undersigned has been designated by the Allied Powers as Supreme Commander for the Allied Powers to carry into effect the general surrender of the Japanese armed forces;

Whereas, the Governments of the United States, Great Britain and Russia at the Moscow Conference, 26th December 1945, having considered the effectuation by Japan of the Terms

183

of Surrender, with the concurrence of China have agreed that the Supreme Commander shall issue all Orders for the implementation of the Terms of Surrender.

Now, therefore, I, Douglas MacArthur, as Supreme Commander for the Allied Powers, by virtue of the authority so conferred upon me, in order to implement the Term of Surrender which requires the meting out of stern justice to war criminals, do order and provide as follows:

Article 1. There shall be established an International Military Tribunal for the Far East for the trial of those persons charged individually, or as members of organizations, or in both capacities, with offenses which include crimes against peace.

Article 2. The Constitution, jurisdiction and functions of this Tribunal are those set forth in the Charter of the International Military Tribunal for the Far East, approved by me this day.

Article 3. Nothing in this Order shall prejudice the jurisdiction of any other international, national or occupation court, commission or other tribunal established or to be established in Japan or in any territory of a United Nation with which Japan has been at war, for the trial of war criminals.

Given under my hand at Tokyo, this 19th day of January, 1946.

Douglas MacArthur
General of the Army, United States Army
Supreme Commander for the Allied Powers

CHARTER OF THE INTERNATIONAL MILITARY TRIBUNAL FOR THE FAR EAST, APRIL 26, 1946

Section I

CONSTITUTION OF TRIBUNAL

Article 1. Tribunal Established. The International Military Tribunal for the Far East is hereby established for the just and prompt trial and punishment of the major war criminals in the Far East. The permanent seat of the Tribunal is in Tokyo.

Article 2. Members. The Tribunal shall consist of not less than six members nor more than eleven members, appointed by the Supreme Commander for the Allied Powers from the names submitted by the Signatories to the Instrument of Surrender, India, and the Commonwealth of the Philippines.

Article 3. Officers and Secretariat.

    a. *President.* The Supreme Commander for the Allied Powers shall appoint a Member to be President of the Tribunal.

    b. *Secretariat.*

        (1) The Secretariat of the Tribunal shall be composed of a General Secretary to be appointed by the Supreme Commander for the Allied Powers and such assistant secretaries, clerks, interpreters, and other personnel as may be necessary.

        (2) The General Secretary shall organize and direct the work of the Secretariat.

        (3) The Secretariat shall receive all documents addressed to the Tribunal, maintain the records of the Tribunal, provide necessary clerical services to the Tribunal and its members, and perform such other duties as may be designated by the Tribunal.

Article 4. Convening and Quorum, Voting, and Absence.

    a. *Convening and Quorum.* When as many as six members of the Tribunal are present, they may convene the Tri-

185

bunal in formal session. The presence of a majority of all members shall be necessary to constitute a quorum.

b. *Voting.* All decisions and judgments of this Tribunal, including convictions and sentences, shall be by a majority vote of those members of the Tribunal present. In case the votes are evenly divided, the vote of the President shall be decisive.

c. *Absence.* If a member at any time is absent and afterwards is able to be present, he shall take part in all subsequent proceedings; unless he declares in open court that he is disqualified by reason of insufficient familiarity with the proceedings which took place in his absence.

Section II

JURISDICTION AND GENERAL PROVISIONS

Article 5. Jurisdiction Over Persons and Offenses. The Tribunal shall have the power to try and punish Far Eastern war criminals who as individuals or as members of organizations are charged with offenses which include Crimes against Peace. The following acts, or any of them, are crimes coming within the jurisdiction of the Tribunal for which there shall be individual responsibility:

a. *Crimes against Peace*: Namely, the planning, preparation, initiation or waging of a declared or undeclared war of aggression, or a war in violation of international law, treaties, agreements or assurances, or participation in a common plan or conspiracy for the accomplishment of any of the foregoing;

b. *Conventional War Crimes*: Namely, violations of the laws or customs of war;

c. *Crimes against Humanity*: Namely, murder, extermination, enslavement, deportation, and other inhumane acts committed before or during the war, or persecutions on political or racial grounds in execution of or in connection with any crime within the jurisdiction of the Tribunal, whether or not in violation of the domestic law of the country where perpetrated. Leaders, organizers, instigators and accomplices participating in the formulation or execution of a common plan or conspiracy to commit any of the foregoing crimes are responsible for all acts performed by any person in execution of such plan.

Article 6. Responsibility of Accused. Neither the official position, at any time, of an accused, nor the fact that an accused acted pursuant to order of his government or of a superior shall, of itself, be sufficient to free such accused from responsibility for any crime with which he is charged, but such circumstances may be considered in mitigation of punishment if the Tribunal determines that justice so requires.

Article 7. Rules of Procedure. The Tribunal may draft and amend rules of procedure consistent with the fundamental provisions of this Charter.

Article 8. Counsel.

a. *Chief of Counsel.* The Chief of Counsel designated by the Supreme Commander for the Allied Powers is responsible for the investigation and prosecution of charges against war criminals within the jurisdiction of this Tribunal and will render such legal assistance to the Supreme Commander as is appropriate.

b. *Associate Counsel.* Any United Nation with which Japan has been at war may appoint an Associate Counsel to assist the Chief of Counsel.

Section III

FAIR TRIAL FOR ACCUSED

Article 9. Procedure for Fair Trial. In order to insure fair trial for the accused the following procedure shall be followed:

a. *Indictment.* The indictment shall consist of a plain,

187

concise, and adequate statement of each offense charged. Each accused shall be furnished, in adequate time for defense, a copy of the indictment, including any amendment, and of this Charter, in a language understood by the accused.

b. *Language.* The trial and related proceedings shall be conducted in English and in the language of the accused. Translations of documents and other papers shall be provided as needed and requested.

c. *Counsel for Accused.* Each accused shall have the right to be represented by counsel of his own selection, subject to the disapproval of such counsel at any time by the Tribunal. The accused shall file with the General Secretary of the Tribunal the name of his counsel. If an accused is not represented by counsel and in open court requests the appointment of counsel, the Tribunal shall designate counsel for him. In the absence of such request the Tribunal may appoint counsel for an accused if in its judgment such appointment is necessary to provide for a fair trial.

d. *Evidence for Defense.* An accused shall have the right, through himself or through his counsel (but not through both), to conduct his defense, including the right to examine any witness, subject to such reasonable restrictions as the Tribunal may determine.

e. *Production of Evidence for the Defense.* An accused may apply in writing to the Tribunal for the production of witnesses or of documents. The application shall state where the witness or document is thought to be located. It shall also state the facts proposed to be proved by the witness or the document and the relevancy of such facts to the defense. If the Tribunal grants the application the Tribunal shall be given such aid in obtaining production of the evidence as the circumstances require.

Article 10. Applications and Motions before Trial. All motions, applications, or other requests addressed to the Tribunal prior to the commencement of trial shall be made in writing and filed with the General Secretary of the Tribunal for action by the Tribunal.

Section IV

POWERS OF TRIBUNAL AND CONDUCT OF TRIAL

Article 11. Powers. The Tribunal shall have the power:

a. To summon witnesses to the trial, to require them to attend and testify, and to question them.

b. To interrogate each accused and to permit comment on his refusal to answer any question.

c. To require the production of documents and other evidentiary material.

d. To require of each witness an oath, affirmation, or such declaration as is customary in the country of the witness, and to administer oaths.

e. To appoint officers for the carrying out of any task designated by the Tribunal, including the power to have evidence taken on commission.

Article 12. Conduct of Trial. The Tribunal shall:

a. Confine the trial strictly to an expeditious hearing of the issues raised by the charges.

b. Take strict measures to prevent any action which would cause any unreasonable delay and rule out irrelevant issues and statements of any kind whatsoever.

c. Provide for the maintenance of order at the trial and deal summarily with any contumacy, imposing appropriate punishment, including exclusion of any accused or his counsel from some or all further proceedings, but without prejudice to the determination of the charges.

d. Determine the mental and physical capacity of any accused to proceed to trial.

Article 13. Evidence.

a. *Admissibility.* The Tribunal shall not be bound by technical rules of evidence. It shall adopt and apply to the greatest possible extent expeditious and non-technical procedure, and shall admit any evidence which it deems to have probative value. All purported admissions or statements of the accused are admissible.

b. *Relevance.* The Tribunal may require to be informed of the nature of any evidence before it is offered in order to rule upon the relevance.

c. *Specific evidence admissible.* In particular, and without limiting in any way the scope of the foregoing general rules, the following evidence may be admitted:

(1) A document, regardless of its security classification and without proof of its issuance or signature, which appears to the Tribunal to have been signed or issued by any officer, department, agency or member of the armed forces of any government.

(2) A report which appears to the Tribunal to have been signed or issued by the International Red Cross or a member thereof, or by a doctor of medicine or any medical service personnel, or by an investigator or intelligence officer, or by any other person who appears to the Tribunal to have personal knowledge of the matters contained in the report.

(3) An affidavit, deposition or other signed statement.

(4) A diary, letter or other document, including sworn or unsworn statements, which appear to the Tribunal to contain information relating to the charge.

(5) A copy of a document or other secondary evidence of its contents, if the original is not immediately available.

d. *Judicial Notice.* The Tribunal shall neither require proof of facts of common knowledge, nor of the authenticity of official government documents and reports of any nation or of the proceedings, records, and findings of military or other agencies of any of the United Nations.

e. *Records, Exhibits, and Documents.* The transcript of the proceedings, and exhibits and documents submitted to the Tribunal, will be filed with the General Secretary of the Tribunal and will constitute part of the Record.

Article 14. Place of Trial. The first trial will be held in Tokyo, and any subsequent trials will be held at such places as the Tribunal decides.

Article 15. Course of Trial Proceedings. The proceedings of the Trial will take the following course:

a. The indictment will be read in court unless the reading is waived by all accused.

b. The Tribunal will ask each accused whether he pleads "guilty" or "not guilty."

c. The prosecution and each accused (by counsel only, if represented) may make a concise opening statement.

d. The prosecution and defense may offer evidence, and the admissibility of the same shall be determined by the Tribunal.

e. The prosecution and each accused (by counsel only, if represented) may examine each witness and each accused who gives testimony.

f. Accused (by counsel only, if represented) may address the Tribunal.

g. The prosecution may address the Tribunal.

h. The Tribunal will deliver judgment and pronounce sentence.

Section V

JUDGMENT AND SENTENCE

Article 16. Penalty. The Tribunal shall have the power to impose upon an accused, on conviction, death, or such other punishment as shall be determined by it to be just.

Article 17. Judgment and Review. The judgment will be announced in open court and will give the reasons on which it is based. The record of the trial will be transmitted directly to the Supreme Commander for the Allied Powers for his action. Sentence will be carried out in accordance with the Order of the Supreme Commander for the Allied Powers, who may at any time reduce or otherwise alter the sentence, except to increase its severity.

By command of General MacArthur:

Richard J. Marshall
Major General, General Staff Corps,
Chief of Staff

2.

JUDGMENT OF THE INTER-
NATIONAL MILITARY TRIBUNAL
FOR THE FAR EAST: FINDINGS ON
COUNTS OF THE INDICTMENT

IN COUNT I of the Indictment it is charged that all the defendants together with other persons participated in the formulation or execution of a common plan or conspiracy. The object of that common plan is alleged to have been that Japan should secure the military, naval, political and economic domination of East Asia and of the Pacific and Indian Oceans, and of all countries and islands therein or bordering thereon, and for that purpose should, alone or in combination with other countries having similar objects, wage a war or wars of aggression against any country or countries which might oppose that purpose.

There are undoubtedly declarations by some of those who are alleged to have participated in the conspiracy which coincide with the above grandiose statement, but in our opinion it has not been proved that these were ever more than declarations of the aspirations of individuals. Thus, for example, we do not think the conspirators ever seriously resolved to attempt to secure the domination of North and South America. So far as the wishes of the conspirators crystallised into a concrete common plan we are of opinion that the territory they had resolved that Japan should dominate was confined to East Asia, the Western and South Western Pacific Ocean and the Indian Ocean, and certain of the islands in these oceans. We shall accordingly treat Count I as if the charge had been limited to the above object.

We shall consider in the first place whether a conspiracy with the above object has been proved to have existed.

Already prior to 1928 Okawa, one of the original defendants, who has been discharged from this trial on account of his present mental state, was publicly advocating that Japan should extend her territory on the Continent of Asia by the threat or, if necessary, by use of military force. He also advocated that Japan should seek to dominate Eastern Siberia and the South Sea Islands. He predicted that the course he advocated must result in a war between the East and the West, in which Japan would be the champion of the East. He was encouraged and aided in his advocacy of this plan by the Japanese General Staff. The object of this plan as stated was substantially the object of the conspiracy, as we have defined it. In our review of the facts we have noticed many subsequent declarations of the conspirators as to the object of the conspiracy. These do not vary in any material respect from this early declaration by Okawa.

Already when Tanaka was premier, from 1927 to 1929, a party of military men, with Okawa and other civilian supporters, was advocating this policy of Okawa's that Japan should expand by the use of force. The conspiracy was now in being. It remained in being until Japan's defeat in 1945. The immediate question when Tanaka was premier was whether Japan should attempt to expand her influence on the continent—beginning with Manchuria—by peaceful penetration, as Tanaka and the members of his Cabinet wished, or whether that expansion should be accomplished by the use of force if necessary, as the conspirators advocated. It was essential that the conspirators should have the support and control of the nation. This was the beginning of the long struggle between the conspirators, who advocated the attainment of their object by force, and those politicians and latterly those bureaucrats, who advocated Japan's expansion by peaceful measures

194

or at least by a more discreet choice of the occasions on which force should be employed. This struggle culminated in the conspirators obtaining control of the organs of government of Japan and preparing and regimenting the nation's mind and material resources for wars of aggression designed to achieve the object of the conspiracy. In overcoming the opposition the conspirators employed methods which were entirely unconstitutional and at times wholly ruthless. Propaganda and persuasion won many to their side, but military action abroad without Cabinet sanction or in defiance of Cabinet veto, assassination of opposing leaders, plots to overthrow by force of arms Cabinets which refused to cooperate with them, and even a military revolt which seized the capital and attempted to overthrow the government were part of the tactics whereby the conspirators came ultimately to dominate the Japanese polity.

As and when they felt strong enough to overcome opposition at home and latterly when they had finally overcome all such opposition the conspirators carried out in succession the attacks necessary to effect their ultimate object, that Japan should dominate the Far East. In 1931 they launched a war of aggression against China and conquered Manchuria and Jehol. By 1934 they had commenced to infiltrate into North China, garrisoning the land and setting up puppet governments designed to serve their purposes. From 1937 onwards they continued their aggressive war against China on a vast scale, overrunning and occupying much of the country, setting up puppet governments on the above model, and exploiting China's economy and natural resources to feed the Japanese military and civilian needs.

In the meantime they had long been planning and preparing a war of aggression which they proposed to launch against the U.S.S.R. The intention was to seize that country's Eastern territories when a favorable opportunity occurred. They had also long recognized that their exploitation of East Asia and their designs on the islands in the Western and South Western Pacific would bring them into conflict with the United States of America, Britain, France and the Netherlands who would defend their threatened interests and territories. They planned and prepared for war against these countries also.

The conspirators brought about Japan's alliance with Germany and Italy, whose policies were as aggressive as their own, and whose support they desired both in the diplomatic and military fields, for their aggressive actions in China had drawn on Japan the condemnation of the League of Nations and left her friendless in the councils of the world.

Their proposed attack on the U.S.S.R. was postponed from time to time for various reasons, among which were (1) Japan's preoccupation with the war in China, which was absorbing unexpectedly large military resources, and (2) Germany's pact of nonaggression with the U.S.S.R., in 1939, which for the time freed the U.S.S.R. from threat of attack on her Western frontier, and might have allowed her to devote the bulk of her strength to the defence of her Eastern territories if Japan had attacked her.

Then in the year 1940 came Germany's great military successes on the continent of Europe. For the time being Great Britain, France and the Netherlands were powerless to afford adequate protection to their interests and territories in the Far East. The military preparations of the United States were in the initial stages. It seemed to the conspirators that no such favorable opportunity could readily recur of realizing that part of their objective which sought Japan's domination of South-West Asia and the islands in the Western and South Western Pacific and Indian Oceans. After prolonged negotiations with the United States of America, in which they refused to disgorge any substantial part of the fruits they had seized as the result of their war of aggression against China, on 7th December 1941 the conspirators launched a war of aggression against the United States and the British Commonwealth. They had already issued orders declaring that a state of war existed between Japan and the Netherlands as from 00.00 hours on 7th December 1941. They had previously secured a jumping-off place for their attacks on the Philippines, Malaya and the Netherlands East Indies by forcing their troops into French Indo-China under threat of military action if this facility was refused to them. Recognizing the existence of a state of war and faced by the imminent threat of invasion of her Far Eastern territories, which the conspirators had long planned and were now about to execute, the Netherlands in self-defence declared war on Japan.

These far-reaching plans for waging wars of aggression, and the prolonged and intricate preparation for and waging of these wars of aggression were not the work of one man. They were the work of many leaders acting in pursuance of a common plan for the achievement of a common object. That common object, that they should secure Japan's domination by preparing and waging wars of aggression, was a criminal object. Indeed no more grave crimes can be conceived of than a conspiracy to wage a war of aggression or the waging of a war of aggression, for the conspiracy threatens the security of the peoples of the world, and the waging disrupts it. The probable result of such a conspiracy, and the inevitable result of its execution is that death and suffering will be inflicted on countless human beings.

The Tribunal does not find it necessary to consider whether there was a conspiracy to wage wars in violation of the treaties, agreements and assurances specified in the particulars annexed to Count 1. The conspiracy to wage wars of aggression was already criminal in the highest degree.

The Tribunal finds that the existence of the criminal conspiracy to wage wars of aggression as alleged in Count 1, with the limitation as to object already mentioned, has been proved.

The question whether the defendants or any of them partici-

197

pated in that conspiracy will be considered when we deal with the individual cases.

The conspiracy existed for and its execution occupied a period of many years. Not all of the conspirators were parties to it at the beginning, and some of those who were parties to it had ceased to be active in its execution before the end. All of those who at any time were parties to the criminal conspiracy or who at any time with guilty knowledge played a part in its execution are guilty of the charge contained in Count 1.

In view of our finding on Count 1 it is unnecessary to deal with Counts 2 and 3, which charge the formulation or execution of conspiracies with objects more limited than that which we have found proved under Count 1, or with Count 4, which charges the same conspiracy as Count 1 but with more specification.

Count 5 charges a conspiracy wider in extent and with even more grandiose objects than that charged in Count 1. We are of opinion that although some of the conspirators clearly desired the achievement of these grandiose objects nevertheless there is not sufficient evidence to justify a finding that the conspiracy charged in Count 5 has been proved.

For the reasons given in an earlier part of this judgment we consider it unnecessary to make any pronouncement on Counts 6 to 26 and 37 to 53. There remain therefore only Counts 27 to 36 and 54 and 55, in respect of which we now give our findings.

Counts 27 to 36 charge the crime of waging wars of aggression and wars in violation of international law, treaties, agreements and assurances against the countries named in those counts.

In the statement of facts just concluded we have found that wars of aggression were waged against all those countries with the exception of the Commonwealth of the Philippines (Count 30) and the Kingdom of Thailand (Count 34). With reference to the Philippines, as we have heretofore stated, that Commonwealth during the period of the war was not a completely sovereign State and so far as international relations were concerned it was a part of the United States of America. We further stated that it is beyond doubt that a war of aggression was waged in the Philippines, but for the sake of technical accuracy we consider the aggressive war in the Philippines as being a part of the war of aggression waged against the United States of America.

Count 28 charges the waging of a war of aggression against the Republic of China over a lesser period of time than that charged in Count 27. Since we hold that the fuller charge contained in Count 27 has been proved we shall make no pronouncement on Count 28.

Wars of aggression having been proved, it is unnecessary to consider whether they were also wars otherwise in violation of international law or in violation of treaties, agreements and assurances. The Tribunal finds therefore that it has been proved that wars of aggression were waged as alleged in Counts 27, 29, 31, 32, 33, 35 and 36.

Count 54 charges ordering, authorizing and permitting the commission of Conventional War Crimes. Count 55 charges failure to take adequate steps to secure the observance and prevent breaches of conventions and laws of war in respect of prisoners of war and civilian internees. We find that there have been cases in which crimes under both those Counts have been proved.

Consequent upon the foregoing findings, we proposed to consider the charges against individual defendants in respect only of the following Counts: Numbers 1, 27, 29, 31, 32, 33, 35, 36, 54 and 55.

3.

DEFENDANTS, VERDICTS, AND SENTENCES

I. Defendants

ARAKI SADAO
General; Army Minister, 1931-1934; Education Minister, 1938-1939.

DOIHARA KENJI
General; Commander-in-Chief, Japanese 5th Army in Manchuria, 1938-1940.

HASHIMOTO KINGORO
Colonel; attached to Army General Staff, 1933; propagandist.

HATA SHUNROKU
General; Commander-in-Chief, Expeditionary Force in Central China, 1940-1944.

HIRANUMA KIICHIRO
Baron; rightist leader, founder of *Kokuhonsha*; President, Privy Council, 1936-1939; Prime Minister, 1939.

HIROTA KOKI
Career diplomat; Foreign Minister, 1933-1936; Prime Minister, 1936-1937.

HOSHINO NAOKI
Bureaucrat; President, Planning Board, 2nd Konoe cabinet; Chief Secretary and Minister without Portfolio, Tojo cabinet.

ITAGAKI SEISHIRO
General; Chief of Staff, Kwantung Army, 1936-1937; War Minister, 1938-1939.

KAYA OKINORI
Bureaucrat; Minister of Finance, 1937-1938, 1941-1944; President, North China Development Company, 1939-1941.

KIDO KOICHI   Bureaucrat; Education Minister, 1937; Welfare Minister, 1938; Home Minister, 1939; Privy Seal, 1940-1945.

KIMURA HEITARO   General; Vice War Minister, 1941-1944.

KOISO KUNIAKI   General; Chief of Staff, Kwantung Army, 1932-1934; Overseas Minister, 1939-1940; Prime Minister, 1944-1945.

MATSUI IWANE   General; Commander-in-Chief, Japanese Forces in Central China, 1937-1938.

MATSUOKA YOSUKE   Career diplomat; Foreign Minister, 1940-1941.

MINAMI JIRO   General; War Minister, 1931; Commander-in-Chief, Kwantung Army, 1934-1936; Governor-General, Korea, 1936-1942.

MUTO AKIRA   General; Chief, Military Affairs Bureau, War Ministry, 1939-1942; field commands in Dutch East Indies and Philippines, 1943-1945.

NAGANO OSAMI   Admiral; Navy Minister, 1936-1937; Chief of Naval General Staff, 1941-1944.

OKA TAKASUMI   Admiral; Chief, General and Military Affairs Bureau, Navy Ministry, 1940-1944.

OKAWA SHUMEI   Civilian; alleged organizer, Mukden Incident, 1931; propagandist.

OSHIMA HIROSHI   Army officer; Military Attache, Berlin, 1936; Ambassador to Germany, 1938-1939, 1941-1945.

SATO KENRYO	General; Chief, Military Affairs Bureau, War Ministry, 1942-1944.
SHIGEMITSU MAMORU	Career diplomat; Foreign Minister, 1943-1945.
SHIMADA SHIGETARO	Admiral; Navy Minister, 1941-1944.
SHIRATORI TOSHIO	Career diplomat; Ambassador to Italy, 1939.
SUZUKI TEIICHI	General; President, Cabinet Planning Board and Minister without Portfolio, 1941-1943.
TOGO SHIGENORI	Career diplomat; Ambassador to Germany, 1937; Ambassador to U.S.S.R., 1938; Foreign Minister, 1941-1942, 1945.
TOJO HIDEKI	General; Prime Minister and Army Minister, 1941-1944.
UMEZU YOSHIJIRO	General; Commander, Kwantung Army and Ambassador to Manchukuo, 1939-1944.

SOURCES: *Indictment*, Appendix E (*Trial of Japanese War Criminals*, 97-104); Horwitz, "Tokyo Trial," Appendix B, 578-583.

NOTE: Matsuoka and Nagano died during the trial; Okawa was held to be unfit for trial. No verdict was handed down on these three defendants.

II. Verdicts and Sentences

Count	1	27	29	31	32	33	35	36	54	55	Sentence
ARAKI	G	G	A	A	A	A	A	A	A	A	Life Imprisonment
DOIHARA	G	G	G	G	G	A	G	G	G	O	Hanging
HASHIMOTO	G	G	A	A	A				A	A	Life Imprisonment
HATA	G	G	G	G	G		A	A	A	G	Life Imprisonment
HIRANUMA	G	G	G	G	G	A	A	G	A	A	Life Imprisonment
HIROTA	G	G	A	A	A	A	A		A	G	Hanging
HOSHINO	G	G	G	G	G	A	A		A	A	Life Imprisonment
ITAGAKI	G	G	G	G	G	A	G	G	G	O	Hanging
KAYA	G	G	G	G	G				A	A	Life Imprisonment
KIDO	G	G	G	G	G	A	A	A	A	A	Life Imprisonment
KIMURA	G	G	G	G	G				G	G	Hanging
KOISO	G	G	G	G	G			A	A	G	Life Imprisonment
MATSUI	A	A	A	A	A		A	A	A	G	Hanging
MINAMI	G	G	A	A	A				A	A	Life Imprisonment
MUTO	G	G	G	G	G	A		A	G	G	Hanging
OKA	G	G	G	G	G				A	A	Life Imprisonment
OSHIMA	G	A	A	A	A				A	A	Life Imprisonment
SATO	G	G	G	G	G				A	A	Life Imprisonment
SHIGEMITSU	A	G	G	G	G	G	A		A	G	7 Years Imprisonment
SHIMADA	G	G	G	G	G				A	A	Life Imprisonment
SHIRATORI	G	A	A	A	A						Life Imprisonment
SUZUKI	G	G	G	G	G		A	A	A	A	Life Imprisonment
TOGO	G	G	G	G	G			A	A	A	20 Years Imprisonment
TOJO	G	G	G	G	G	G		A	G	O	Hanging
UMEZU	G	G	G	G	G			A	A	A	Life Imprisonment

KEY: Blank--Not indicted on the count.
        G   --Guilty.
        A   --Acquitted.
        O   --Charged but no finding made by the Tribunal.

Count 1 --The Over-all Conspiracy.
Count 27--Waging war against China.
Count 29--Waging war against the United States.
Count 31--Waging war against the British Commonwealth.
Count 32--Waging war against the Netherlands.
Count 33--Waging war against France.
Count 35--Waging war against USSR at Lake Khassan.
Count 36--Waging war against USSR at Nomonhan.
Count 54--Ordering, authorizing or permitting atrocities.
Count 55--Disregard of duty to secure observance of and
          prevent breaches of Laws of War.

SOURCE: Chart taken from Horwitz, "Tokyo Trial," Appendix C, *International Conciliation*, No. 465 (November 1950), p. 584. Used with the permission of the Carnegie Endowment for International Peace.

4.

DEFENSE APPEAL TO GENERAL MacARTHUR

November 21, 1948
To the Supreme Commander for the Allied Powers:

Availing themselves of permission granted, defence counsel for all defendants convicted by the International Military Tribunal for the Far East present this memorandum of points of general applicability. These points have all been treated more fully in the petitions filed on behalf of the defendants individually; here we attempt in the briefest possible compass to sum up the general principles involved.

The Trial was Unfair

The prosecution did not present its case fairly; the Tribunal did not allow the defendants a fair trial. The Chief Prosecutor is reported by the press as having admitted that he prosecuted defendants who were "felt to be of the same mind as us of the United States"—but they were prosecuted, and the death penalty was demanded for all. The Tribunal established rules of procedure for the prosecution, changed them and made them more strict when the defence was being presented, and changed them back again when the prosecution's evidence in rebuttal was offered. The Tribunal refused to hear certain defences which were pleaded, but in its verdict says that those defences cannot be sustained "because there is no evidence to support" them. The Tribunal accepted from the prosecution "evidence" in the form of newspaper reports, second and third-hand rumors and hearsay, opinions of self-styled "experts," and made its findings and verdict on the basis of such "evidence"; it ignored all defence evidence in its verdict, saying that the evidence of Japanese witnesses (although not those who testified for the prosecution) was unsatisfactory and unreliable.

Judges of the Tribunal, in dissenting opinions, have pointed out the unfairness of the proceedings. Mr. Justice Bernard of France, says that "the dispositions of the Charter approved . . . by the Supreme Commander for the Allied Powers, superabundantly manifest their desire to assure the Defendants the maximum guarantees possible. . . . Though I am of opinion that the Charter permitted granting to the accused guarantees sufficient for their defence, I think that actually these were not granted to them"; and he gives concrete examples. Mr. Justice Röling, of The Netherlands, points out instance after instance in which the Tribunal has unfairly construed the evidence, or even ignored it or made findings in the teeth of it. Mr. Justice Pal, of India, has devoted seventy pages of his opinion to the demonstration of the exact way in which the Tribunal's method of procedure and rulings crippled the defence. The President of the Tribunal admits that there was, when the last war started, and is now, much doubt whether aggressive war is a crime.

The Verdict is Not Based on the Evidence

The verdict has been plainly stated by some judges of the Tribunal not to have been based on the evidence; Mr. Justice Bernard has said that he is unable to deny or affirm "that all the evidence and only the evidence produced during the course of the trial was taken into consideration," or that "the points of law and findings of facts adopted by the majority were done so outside of all assistance of persons other than judges." Not only does the verdict give no indication that any of the evidence produced by the defence was taken into consideration, but the great mass of evidence from prosecution witnesses and documents favorable to defendants is never acknowledged; the entire verdict is in the tone of a prosecution's summation, with no favorable reference to any defendant ever admitted. One judge of the majority, who wrote a special opinion to express his insistence on still harsher verdicts, almost confesses his lack of interest in the evidence when he thrice quotes, and emphasizes, the words of the Charter providing for "trial and punishment" of the defendants. Not even of those defendants convicted by a bare majority, and given the rare light sentences, is there a good word in the majority verdict.

Guilt has not been Proved beyond a Reasonable Doubt

The verdict is not that of the Tribunal, but of a clique of it. It has been disclosed that the seven-judge majority excluded from the deliberations and decision not only Messrs. Justices Pal and Bernard, who dissented generally, but Mr. Justice Röling who dissented in part and concurred in part, and the President, Sir William Webb, who expressed grave doubts concerning several points of the result, but recorded no dissent. It is known that death sentences were imposed by vote of six to five in some cases, of seven to four in others, but in no case by vote of more than seven judges. The law of most of the civilized world requires unanimity for imposing a sentence of death, and usually for conviction of a crime; we Americans would consider it an outrage that six or seven men out of eleven should convict and sentence to death, and the community of civilized nations must regard it as an outrage here. Guilt has not been proved beyond a reasonable doubt, but the "doubt" in some cases is so overwhelming that there cannot even be said to be a reasonable doubt of guilt.

The Verdict will not achieve the Allied Powers' Purposes

The purposes of our nations in holding these trials are two; to establish it as the law that aggression is a crime, to be paid for by heavy penalties; and to impress upon our defeated enemies and the world, that our attachment to the law which we are acting in support of is such that we will accord even those enemies a fair trial by judicial process. This verdict must inevitably fail to further either end.

The state of the international law relating to crimes against peace is not clarified, but muddled, by this verdict. The Tribunal produced six separate opinions, from consideration of all of which it is impossible for even an international lawyer to determine what law is being applied. Not only dissenting judges, but judges concurring in the result, have written opinions expressing grave doubts concerning some of the doctrines adopted by the majority, which doctrines in such cases may prove to be those of only a plurality even of this Tribunal; such doctrines as do rest on a clear majority will have little influence on international law, which is based on the consensus of all or an overwhelming majority of civilized nations. If the trial of the military and civilian leaders of defeated nations is to be a normal aftermath of war, for the sake of all of us we had better see to the establishment of definitely fixed law under which to punish them.

The verdict looks too much like an act of vengeance to impress the world with our love of justice and fair play. The conviction of all defendants alike, even those whom the prosecution admits should not have been charged and of those whose conviction they are "ashamed" compares unfavorably with the result of the Nuremberg trial, where guilt or innocence, as well as sentence, were declared individually rather than en masse—even though, as the President of our Tribunal has pointed out, "the crimes of the German accused were far more heinous, varied and extensive than those of the Japanese accused." This verdict looks too much like vindictiveness to impress the Japanese people, who see convicted, all alike, statesmen who were notorious in militaristic Japan for fighting for peace, soldiers who merely entered a war late, men who voiced outspoken opposition to aggression, or who at great risks worked to end the war.

207

And lastly, as to the effect on ourselves—for we who address you are Americans, and if this trial was international, the Supreme Commander whose action is now awaited is an American, and his act will be considered that of America. We can only stultify ourselves if we become party to the use of the forms of law and justice to perpetrate acts of vengeance. We will not impress our enemies; we will not gain the respect of our friends; we will in the end brutalize and destroy ourselves. A hundred and fifty years ago Lord Erskine—that impassioned defender of justice and liberty whose name has outlasted those of all the prosecutors whom he met in the arena—in one of his celebrated defences, speaking of England, put the matter in terms equally applicable to the international community whose course is here involved, and in words of equal significance for our day: "Unjust prosecutions lead to the ruin of all governments. Whoever will look back to the history of the world in general, and of our own particular country, will be convinced that exactly as prosecutions have been cruel and oppressive, and maintained by inadequate and unrighteous evidence, in the same proportion, and by the same means, their authors have been destroyed instead of being supported by them. As often as the principles of our ancient laws have been departed from in weak and wicked times, so often have the governments that have violated them been suddenly crumbled into dust."

If we hope for a world organized under law and operating under the rule of law and the principles of justice, we must not ourselves be guilty of atrocities against the law and justice. No good, but only pyramided evil, will come from the verdict of this Tribunal as it now stands. A fearless act of statesmanship now can salvage much of the prestige which the act of this small group of judges would lose to our countries: we urge that it be performed.

Ben Bruce Blakeney,
On behalf of all Defence Counsel.

5.

MISCELLANEOUS ADDITIONAL CRITICISMS

LEST the reader assume that I have exhausted the possible criticisms of the Tokyo tribunal, let me point out several further items, major and minor.

Consider first the verdicts on Shigemitsu and Togo. The tribunal heard testimony that Shigemitsu entered the Tojo cabinet in April 1943 with the intention of negotiating peace. Nevertheless, the Judgment held his tenure in that cabinet against him (1,195-1,196). See Röling, *Opinion*, pp. 228-242, especially p. 228: "The evidence before this tribunal reveals Shigemitsu as a diplomat and a statesman who worked for peace rather than for war." See also Hankey, *Politics*, pp. 90-110; Shigemitsu Mamoru, *Japan and Her Destiny*, ed. F.S.G. Piggott, tr. Oswald White (New York: Dutton, 1958); and the various testimonials appended to "Petition on behalf of Shigemitsu Mamoru for Review of Judgment, Verdict and Sentence of the International Military Tribunal for the Far East, 18 November 1948, George A. Furness and Hisao Yanai." I am grateful to Mr. Furness for showing me his copy of this petition. Togo had joined the Tojo cabinet to pursue a final attempt at negotiations, yet his tenure in the cabinet was held against him (*Judgment*, pp. 1,204-1,205). See Röling, *Opinion*, pp. 243-249, especially 245: "In the crime against peace, the decisive element is the intention of aggression. If, as the inevitable result of having occupied a position for the sake of promoting peace, one is forced to vote for war, one cannot be accused of aggressive intent." See also Ike, *Japan's Decision for War* and Togo Shigenori, *The Cause of Japan*, tr. and ed., Togo Fumihiko and Ben Bruce Blakeney (New York: Simon and Schuster, 1956).

Consider also some discrepancies in the sentences meted out. Koiso, guilty of the conspiracy, of four counts of aggression, and of "reckless disregard of legal duty," received life imprisonment. Matsui, guilty *only* of "reckless disregard," was sentenced to death. Shigemitsu, guilty of five counts of aggression and of "reckless disregard," received seven years' imprisonment.

Consider further the prosecution's reliance on the Kido diary (see Pal, *Judgment*, pp. 141-142), the Harada-Saionji memoirs (see Pal, *Judgment*, pp. 142-148), and on witness Tanaka Ryukichi. Of Tanaka, Pal wrote that his ". . . services were freely requisitioned by the prosecution to fill in all possible gaps in its evidence. Here is a man who seems to have been very much attractive to every wrongdoer of Japan who, after having committed the act, somehow and some time sought out this man and confided him with his evil doings" (Pal, *Judgment*, p. 225). Even the Judgment criticized Tanaka, calling him ". . . a witness whom both prosecution and defense adduced from time to time, as occasion demanded, and whom both prosecution and defense cross-examined as a witness of no credit, again as occasion demanded" (*Judgment*, p. 653). For some comments on Tanaka's character and motivation, see Butow, *Tojo*, pp. 492-494. For the allegation that Tanaka kept Chief Prosecutor Keenan supplied with wine and women, see Kojima, *Tokyo saiban*, I, 245.

Consider the language problems involved. Although English and Japanese were the official languages, and a language staff designed to cope with these languages existed, many other languages were also in use by witnesses and even by prosecutors (French and Russian). There was even a squabble over classical and colloquial Outer Mongolian. There were constant interruptions of the proceedings by language monitors to correct mistakes in interpretation, and there were frequent challenges to that interpretation from defense and prosecution. The problem of translation between English and Japanese proved at times insurmountable. Robert Butow, after comparing the English and Japanese transcripts, concluded: "It is . . . obvious that a breakdown in communication from one language to the other frequently occurred" (Butow, *Tojo*, pp. 497, 501).

Finally, to descend to the ridiculous, consider the issue of Chief Prosecutor Keenan's sobriety. One spectator at the trial, Courtney Browne, writes: "Evident, too, were the unfortunate occasions when Keenan's naturally florid complexion was flushed more than usual and when he might charitably have been described as being unfit to be in court." (Courtney Browne, *Tojo: The Last Banzai*, New York [Holt, Rinehart and Winston, 1967], p. 255.) See also Butow, *Tojo*, p. 496.

BIBLIOGRAPHICAL NOTE

THE major source for this book is of course the Records of the Tokyo trial itself. These consist of the Proceedings, the verbatim transcript of the trial; the Proceedings in Chambers, the verbatim transcript of the conferences among justices, prosecution counsel, and defense counsel; the various judgments, six in all; and the Proceedings on Review before General MacArthur. Less important for my purpose were the various ancillary exhibits and records prepared by the prosecution and the defense.

When one thinks of the publication in forty-two volumes of the proceedings and judgments of the Nuremberg trial, one is struck immediately by the failure of the U.S. Government to make the materials of the Tokyo trial widely available. Mimeographed copies of the Proceedings have been available from the start, but only at the following libraries: Department of the Army, National Archives, Library of Congress, Harvard Law School, Hoover Institute (at Stanford), and University of California at Berkeley. In addition, the majority judgment was published in November 1948 (no place), and the Indictment and Keenan's Opening Statement was issued by the State Department in 1946 ("Trial of the Japanese War Criminals," State Department Publication, 2613).

Recently, the Proceedings have been put on microfilm by the Library of Congress. This effort may be a duplication, since Horwitz writes of a Department of the Army microfilm (of the Proceedings and the exhibits) available in 1950. In any case, the microfilm copy issued by the Library of Congress does not include the five separate dissenting and concurring opinions, since the tribunal overrode protests and read only the majority judgment in open court. Nor does it include the Proceedings on Review before General MacArthur. These Proceedings are available at the National Archives, but apparently not at the

Library of Congress or at the deposit libraries listed above. The separate opinions of Justices Bernard, Jaranilla, Röling, and Webb are available today only at the deposit libraries. Justice Pal's opinion is the sole exception. It was published commercially in India in 1953.

For description of these trial materials see Solis Horwitz, "The Tokyo Trial" (*International Conciliation*, 465:473-584, November 1950, Appendix A, 576-577). Sung Yoon Cho, "The Tokyo War Crimes Trial," *Quarterly Journal of the Library of Congress*, 24.4:309-318 (October 1967) describes the holdings of the Library of Congress. Charles V. Kirchman and Garry D. Ryan, "Preliminary Inventory of the Textual Records of the International Military Tribunal for the Far East," Record Group 238, General Services Administration, National Archives and Record Service, NM 62 (1965) lists all documents in the collection of the National Archives. Delmer M. Brown, "Instruction and Research: Recent Japanese Political and Historical Materials," *American Political Science Review*, 43.5: 1,010-1,017 (October 1949) surveys materials at the University of California at Berkeley. For an index of the Proceedings, see Paul S. Dull and Michael Takaaki Umemura, *The Tokyo Trials: A Functional Index to the Proceedings of the International Military Tribunal for the Far East*, Ann Arbor: University of Michigan Press (Center for Japanese Studies: Occasional Paper 6), 1957.

Twenty-two years after the trial the only extended treatment of the trial is Solis Horwitz, "The Tokyo Trial." Horwitz was a member of the Prosecution, and his account is heavily biased. (For volume of scholarly treatment, compare again the coverage of Nuremberg.) Shorter treatments of the trial are to be found in: John Alan Appleman, *Military Tribunals and International Crimes* (Indianapolis: Bobbs-Merrill, 1954); Lord Hankey, *Politics, Trials and Errors* (Chicago: Henry Regnery, 1950); Gordon Ireland, "Uncommon Law in Martial Tokyo," *The Year Book of World Affairs*, 4:50-104 (1950); Paul W.

Schroeder, *The Axis Alliance and Japanese-American Relations, 1941* (Ithaca: Cornell University Press, 1958); Paul Chungtseng Tsai, "Judicial Administration of the Laws of War: Procedures in War Crimes Trials," Doctor of Law thesis (Yale, 1957); and Robert K. Woetzel, *The Nuremberg Trials in International Law*, rev. ed. (New York: Praeger, 1962).

Japanese accounts include the following: Asahi shimbun hotei kishadan, *Tokyo saiban*, 3 vols. (Tokyo: Asahi, 1962); Kiyose Ichiro, *Hiroku Tokyo saiban* (Tokyo: Yomiuri, 1967); Kojima Noboru, *Tokyo saiban*, 2 vols. (Tokyo: Chuo koron, 1971), Takayanagi Kenzo, *Kyokuto saiban to kokusaiho* (Tokyo: Yuhikaku, 1948—includes English text under title *The Tokio Trials and International Law*); Takikawa Masajiro, *Tokyo saiban o sabaku* (Tokyo: Towasha, 1952); Tanaka Masaaki, *Pa-ru hakase no Nihon muzairon* (Tokyo: Keibunsha, 1963); Tateno Nobuyuki, *Zoku Nihon senryo* (Tokyo: Kodansha, 1964); Tokyo saiban kenkyukai, ed., *Kyodo kenkyu Paru hanketsusho* (Tokyo: Tokyo saiban kankokai, 1966); and Uematsu Keita, *Kyokuto kokusai gunji saiban* (Tokyo: Jimbutsu oraisha, 1962).

Many participants in the Tokyo trial have written articles. Prominent among these are: George F. Blewett, A. S. Comyns-Carr, Owen Cunningham, Joseph B. Keenan (Keenan also wrote a book with Brendan Francis Brown, *Crimes Against International Law* [Washington: Public Affairs Press, 1950]), A. Frederick Mignone, Justice B.V.A. Röling, David N. Sutton. For exact citations, see footnotes and/or *Index of Periodical Literature*.

Valuable also are the standard treatments of Nuremberg. For a recent bibliography, see Eugene Davidson, *The Trial of the Germans* (New York: Macmillan, 1966), pp. 595-615. Especially useful as parallel critical treatments are: Montgomery Belgion, *Victor's Justice* (Hinsdale: Henry Regnery, 1949); Freda Utley, *The High Cost of Vengeance* (Chicago: Henry Regnery, 1949); and F.J.P. Veale, *Advance to Barbarism* (Appleton: Nelson, 1953).

215

INDEX

Abe Nobuyuki, 104n67, 105, 106, 108n70
accused, *see* defendants
affirmation of justices, 5, 77
aggression: in Indictment, 24-25, 47, 135, 144; Soviet declaration of war on Japan and, 95-99, 134; American-Japanese relations and, 98-99, 144-158; Dutch-Japanese relations and, 99; majority judgment on Japanese, 134-140, 144-148; Pal on American-Japanese relations and, 156-158; Rusk and, 178
aggression, criminality of: Jackson on, 11-12, 47-48, 98-99; defense motion on, 25, 26, 27; majority judgment on, 27-28, 54-55; Pal on, 32, 54, 94; Röling on, 33, 53-54; London Conference and, 43, 47-49, 72, 94; United Nations War Crimes Commission and, 49-50, 72; Keenan on, 50; Takayanagi on, 50-53; Bernard on, 53; United Nations and, 72n85. *See also* conspiracy, crimes against peace, Pact of Paris
aggression, definition of: in Nuremberg Charter, 7; Pact of Paris and, 55; London Conference and, 55-57; Jackson on, 55-57, 98-99, 147; Stone on, 55n51, 56n53; Soviet draft, 56n53; Keenan

on, 57-58; majority judgment on, 58; Röling on, 58-59; Pal on, 59-60, 94, 99; Kellogg on, 59n59. *See also* Pact of Paris
Allied Council for Japan, 33, 164-166, 168
Allies, *see* names of individual states
Appleman, John Alan, 32n27, 83-84, 85n26
Araki Sadao, 200
Arendt, Hannah, 126
Arita Hachirō, 107
associate counsel, *see* International Prosecution Section
atomic bombings, 95, 99-102, 120
Australia, 23, 50, 72n85, 111, 165
Axis, 49, 63, 93-94
Axis alliance, 101n62, 140-144, 153-154, 155

Bataan Death March, 82, 162
Beard, Charles A., 153
Bernard, Henri, 75, 82n18, 86, 92, 165; on procedural flaws, 32, 89-90, 90n42, 125, 140, 162-163; on emperor, 32, 117, 163, 165; on aggressive war, 53, 162; on negative criminality, 70; on qualifications of justices, 78-79; vote of, 91n44; on conspiracy charge, 133; on international community, 139n35; on individual responsibility, 162

217

179, 179n35; trials of
Japanese nationals for, 6,
6n3, 67; and meaning of
term "war criminals," 7, 8,
21, 27; recognized in international law, 16, 34, 62;
Charter and, 21; Indictment
and, 24; majority judgment
on, 31, 71, 135; Pal on, 32,
69. See also conspiracy to
commit conventional war
crimes
Cramer, Myron H., 82-83, 87,
88, 116n85; vote of,
91n44, 102
crimes against humanity, 6, 8,
15, 21, 24, 34-35; defined in
Nuremberg Charter, 7; in
Nuremberg judgment, 7n5;
in Tokyo Charter, 21. See
also murder
crimes against peace, 6, 8, 10,
34, 144, 179n35; defined in
Nuremberg Charter, 7;
Tokyo Charter and, 21, 22;
and murder, 24; defense
challenge on, 26. See also
aggression, Pact of Paris
Cunningham, Owen, 84, 89,
126n3
Czechoslovakia, 49-50

Darrow, Clarence, 38n11
defendants, 4, 6; sentences
against, 5-6, 31, 172; Indictment on, 23, 25; motions in
behalf of, 25, 26-28, 76-77;
verdicts on, 5, 28, 31, 144,
175-176; parole of, 172-
175; Keenan on guilt of,

175n33. See also names of
individual defendants
defendants, choice of, 74-75;
definition of crimes in
Charter and, 93-94; Pal on
definition of crimes and, 94;
Allied war crimes and,
94-102; Keenan on criteria
for, 102; Horwitz on criteria
for, 103, 103n66, 104n67;
original decision on, 104-106;
and omission of Kishi, 106-
107; and omission of Yonai
and Arita, 107; Soviet Union
and, 107-109; and omission
of industrialist, 110; and
omission of emperor,
110-113, 116-117
defense counsel, 80, 147,
165n11; composition of, 4-5,
23; provision of Charter for,
22, 23n8; motions by, 25,
26-28; abuse of, 83-84,
85n26; petition to MacArthur
of, 90-91, 161, 164; Keenan's
criticism of, 175n33; text of
petition to MacArthur of,
204-208
Dennis et al. vs. United States,
37n9
Doihara Kenji, 200
Douglas, William O., 66,
170-172
Dulles, John Foster, 173
Dutch East Indies, 147

Ehrlichman, John D., 179n35
Eichmann, Adolf, xi, 169
El Salvador, 174
emperor, role of, 113-116;

219